ADVANCE PRAISE

"Recovering from infidelity is hard work. Dr. Erb helps us with her professional experience, her biblical understanding, her realism, and doesn't paste a Bible verse over a hurting heart or expect the betrayed to pretend all is well. Do you want to grow through your experience of infidelity or become hard and bitter? Dr. Erb has given us a very helpful workbook for those who have been deeply betrayed by a spouse. I wish I'd had it years ago when I discovered my husband's infidelity. I commend this workbook to you to help you through the recovery process." ~**Ruth Graham,** *In Every Pew Sits a Broken Heart*

"Dr. Erb's workbook gives hope for women who have been wounded by their husbands. Who better to help them than a person who has walked in their shoes? Also, understanding that other women have been wounded by their husbands will give them the courage to face this betrayal, learn to trust God and move forward with their lives. It will help them learn how to deal with their emotions and understand the four stages of emotional healing.

This workbook will also teach them that God created each of them uniquely and that each wounded woman will walk through their grief and emotional healing at their own pace. They will learn to draw closer to the Lord, take their mind off their circumstances, let go of their anger, and forgive the husband who has wounded them. When they do this, the Lord will comfort them, guide them, and lead them to emotional healing. Romans 8:31b tells us: "...If God be for us, who can be against us." ~**Dr. Phyllis Arno, co-founder of the National Christian Counselors Association**

"Dr. Carol Erb knows betrayal. Dr. Carol Erb knows the Bible. Dr. Carol Erb knows how to help a wife get through the pain and confusion of betrayal to full healing and recovery. If your husband has had an affair, get this workbook!" ~**Dr. David Clarke, Christian psychologist and author of** *I Don't Want a Divorce*

"From Betrayal to Healing is more than a workbook. It's a journey toward healing for any woman experiencing the pain and loss that comes from marital infidelity. Carol Erb masterfully weaves together important spiritual truths with practical steps, guiding the reader from the moment of impact to a place of hope. The exercises and introspective questions in each chapter allow the reader critical insight into her personal progress along the way. From Betrayal to Healing is a must-have resource for both counselors and clients!" ~**Stephanie Baker, MA, speaker, co-author and executive director of Life in Abundance counseling ministry**

FROM BETRAYAL TO HEALING

Begin Healing from Your Husband's Affair

CAROL ERB, Ph.D.

Copyright © 2018 Carol Erb. All rights reserved. No portion of this book may be reproduced mechanically, electronically, or by any other means, including photocopying, without written permission from the author. It is illegal to copy this book, post it to a website, or distribute it by any other means without permission from the author.

Author Contact: drcarolerb.com

Thomas Noble Books
Wilmington, DE
www.thomasnoblebooks.com
Library of Congress Control Number: 2018943117
ISBN: 978-1-945586-11-8
First Printing: 2018
Editing by Gwen Hoffnagle
Cover Design by Rebecca Barnheart of yourbusinessdesigner.com

This publication is designed to provide accurate and authoritative information regarding the subject matter covered. It is sold with the understanding that the author is not engaged in rendering professional services in this publication. If legal, accounting, medical, psychological, or any other expert assistance is required, the services of a competent professional person should be sought. Client names have been changed to protect identities.

DEDICATION

For all the women who have invited me to walk with them on their journey from betrayal to healing. Your courage, faith, and strength are inspiring.

"For I know the plans that I have for you," declares the LORD, "plans for welfare and not for calamity to give you a future and a hope."

–Jeremiah 29:11

ACKNOWLEDGEMENTS

To my husband, Walt – Since I wrote my first book, *Enveloped*, you continually said a workbook needed to be written for women who have been betrayed by a husband's affair. It needed to be a special book for individuals, counselors, and ministry leaders to use. God's timing has arrived. Thank you for encouraging me in my writing, speaking, and counseling. I have been truly blessed by your faith and devotion. You are God's gift to me.

To my business and design coach, Rebecca Barnheart – God sovereignly chose you to help me bring my vision to the online world so that more women can be helped and healed. You've shown me the perfect balance of perseverance and patience. I couldn't have done it without you.

To my publisher, Lynne Klippel, of Thomas Noble Books – Once again you took my project and ran with it. You encouraged me to take what I had created for my private practice clients and make it available to the general public. You believed in me from our very first phone call. You are a Godsend.

To my editor, Gwen Hoffnagle – Thank you for making my readers your priority and helping me deliver my message with clarity. You have an incredible eye for detail and always exceed my expectations.

To Dr. Phyllis Arno and the National Christian Counselors Association family – Thank you for your faithfulness and assistance in helping me fulfill my call into Christian counseling. Your encouragement to write this book and willingness to offer recommendations in the area of temperament has been invaluable.

To my Wonderful Counselor and Comforter – Truly, Lord, you show everlasting lovingkindness and have great compassion for all who have been betrayed because you experienced it too. I give you each woman you send, knowing you are her true Healer.

He heals the brokenhearted and binds up their wounds.

−Psalm 147:3

Table of Contents

Introduction 10

Lesson 1: Dealing with Emotions 15

Lesson 2: Identifying Losses 37

Lesson 3: Facing Anger 55

Lesson 4: Battling Depression 69

Lesson 5: Preparing for Disclosure 83

Lesson 6: Understanding Boundaries 97

Lesson 7: Confronting Fears 107

Lesson 8: Understanding the 'Why' of His Affair 115

Lesson 9: Releasing Resentment 129

Lesson 10: Forgiving Him 139

Lesson 11: Rebuilding Trust 151

Lesson 12: Believing God 163

About the Author 179

Connect with Carol 180

INTRODUCTION

Welcome, my sister in betrayal. Because you picked up this workbook, I assume we have something in common – we've both been betrayed by our husband's affair.

Many years ago I discovered that my husband, a loving man and devoted father, was not who I thought. He was having an affair with a young woman nearly half my age. I was in disbelief, devastated, and worried about what his betrayal would mean for our three sons and for me. My husband walked out and I had to acquiesce to a divorce. It felt like my world was falling apart. The only hope I could cling to was my faith in God.

God led me through that dark time on a path of healing that changed my life completely. Today I am a Christian counselor and marriage coach dedicated to helping women, especially Christian women, heal from their husbands' affairs. They are feeling overwhelmed and betrayed and don't know what to do next. I help them rebuild their confidence, reignite their faith, and remove their fear of the future so they can trust their decisions and take the next right step in their marriages and their lives.

I'm happily remarried to a wonderful, faithful man named Walt. He has been my partner in life and love for the past thirteen years. I'm telling you my story so that you'll know healing is possible.

Matthew 19:26 says,

> *"With God, all things are possible."*

That verse has been proven in my life and the lives of thousands of women I've helped over the past fifteen years.

This workbook walks you through the process I use in my private practice. You can work through the material on your own, in a support group, with a counselor, or with me. I work with women privately by phone, by video call, and in online group programs.

The goal is to help you restore your trust in yourself and in God's loving provision for your life. You may be able to reconcile with your husband, and I hope that's possible. Or you may realize it's necessary to move on to a new future on your own. That decision is between you and God, and He will guide you. No one else can make that decision for you. Whatever choice you make, the information in this workbook will help you embrace that a good life is waiting for you and that you deserve it!

There are twelve lessons in this workbook. My suggestion is that you complete one each week so that you have time to reflect on it and listen for God's direction and encouragement in between lessons. However, you can set your own pace and the rhythm that works best for you.

I want you to write in this book!

I know you might find that hard to do, especially if you were taught to never write in a book. But this is a workbook designed for you to use. Fill in the pages with your ideas, bend down the corners of the ones that mean the most to you, use your highlighter, draw pictures, and let this book become a receptacle for your thoughts, emotions, and hopes for the future. Don't worry if you spill your coffee or tea on a few pages or if some become tearstained. This is a book to use, not to let gather dust on your bookshelf.

If you have children at home, store this workbook in a private place where they will not read it. And keep it private from your husband for now. This is your workbook and a safe place for you to express all your feelings, even the painful ones.

To begin our work together, I would like you to write about your husband's betrayal and what it did to you. It is important to write down the story so you can stop carrying it around as a burden on your heart and begin the healing process. Imagine that I am sitting beside you in your kitchen having coffee and listening to your story. Don't hold back.

Lesson 1
Dealing with Emotions

Lesson 1: Dealing with Emotions

In this lesson you will:

- Learn the four stages of emotional healing
- Learn to identify your emotions
- Review the most common reactions to a husband's affair
- Differentiate between supportive and unsupportive people
- Begin to identify your boundaries
- Open yourself up to receive God's love despite your pain

When you discover that your husband has had an affair, you can have several responses including:

- Can't believe he'd do this to you
- Blame other people or the environment
- Think your marriage was all a lie
- Can't have sex without thinking about his affair with his betrayal partner
- Feel exhausted and want to sleep all the time
- Work harder and longer
- Want him to move out
- Withdraw from friends and social activities
- Find it difficult to focus and finish tasks
- Blame yourself and wonder why he didn't tell you he wasn't happy
- Link your feelings to your husband: when he is doing better, you are better
- Stay stuck in anger and not be able to forgive
- Want to hurry up and get past it
- Believe your husband when he says he will never cheat again
- Secretly think about getting involved with someone else yourself to meet your emotional and sexual needs

These reactions are common. Let's explore them:

How do you deny or minimize what has happened?

Do you make excuses, or pretend everything is okay?

How are you avoiding this situation?

If you avoid sharing the situation with others, do you use your time to rest and recover in a healthy way or are you avoiding others out of shame or embarrassment?

If you're ashamed or embarrassed, why?

Who do you blame for this situation?

From Betrayal to Healing

If you blame yourself at all, in what ways are you to blame?

Have you made some unhealthy choices that might have led to this?

No matter how you answered these questions, you are not at fault for your husband's affair! You didn't push your husband into the arms of another person. That is his sin, not yours. We all dislike things about ourselves and think we should change. You're aware of mistakes you've made in your marriage. However, his affair didn't happen because you gained weight, got older, or were too busy with the responsibilities of your life.

Has your husband said that he will change? What did he say?

Do his actions match his words?

It is very important that you judge your husband by what he does, not what he says. If he says he wants to change and be forgiven to preserve your marriage, do his actions match up with those words?

You don't have to rush to make a decision about the future of your marriage. Wait and see. Pray and ask God to reveal His plan for you. Observe your husband's actions and see if he can maintain positive, faithful behaviors over time.

The Four Stages of Emotional Healing

Whenever we have a tragedy in our lives, and your husband's affair is certainly a tragedy, we move through four different stages of grief and emotional healing.

They are:

- Shock
- Tangled emotions
- Disorientation
- Acceptance and Rebuilding

Which stage do you feel you are in today? Why?

It's interesting that grief doesn't work in a straight line. It's more like a spiral. Some days you feel better and like you're healing, and the next day the shock and pain hits you hard again.

There is no right or wrong way to grieve the loss of trust and fidelity in your marriage, but don't ignore the process. Give yourself the time and space to grieve and fully feel your emotions. That is the best path to acceptance and rebuilding.

From Betrayal to Healing

What have you lost since learning about your husband's infidelity?

How do you feel about these losses today?

What can you do to heal from some of these losses?

How can you be kind to yourself as you walk through this time of sadness and loss?

Identifying Your Emotions

Many of the women I counsel have a hard time figuring out exactly what they are feeling other than pain. That pain is so overwhelming that it feels like a big ball of fire. However, that pain has many layers to it.

Look at the Emotion Wheel on the next page and notice all the emotions that contribute to your feelings of pain.

Begin Healing from Your Husband's Affair

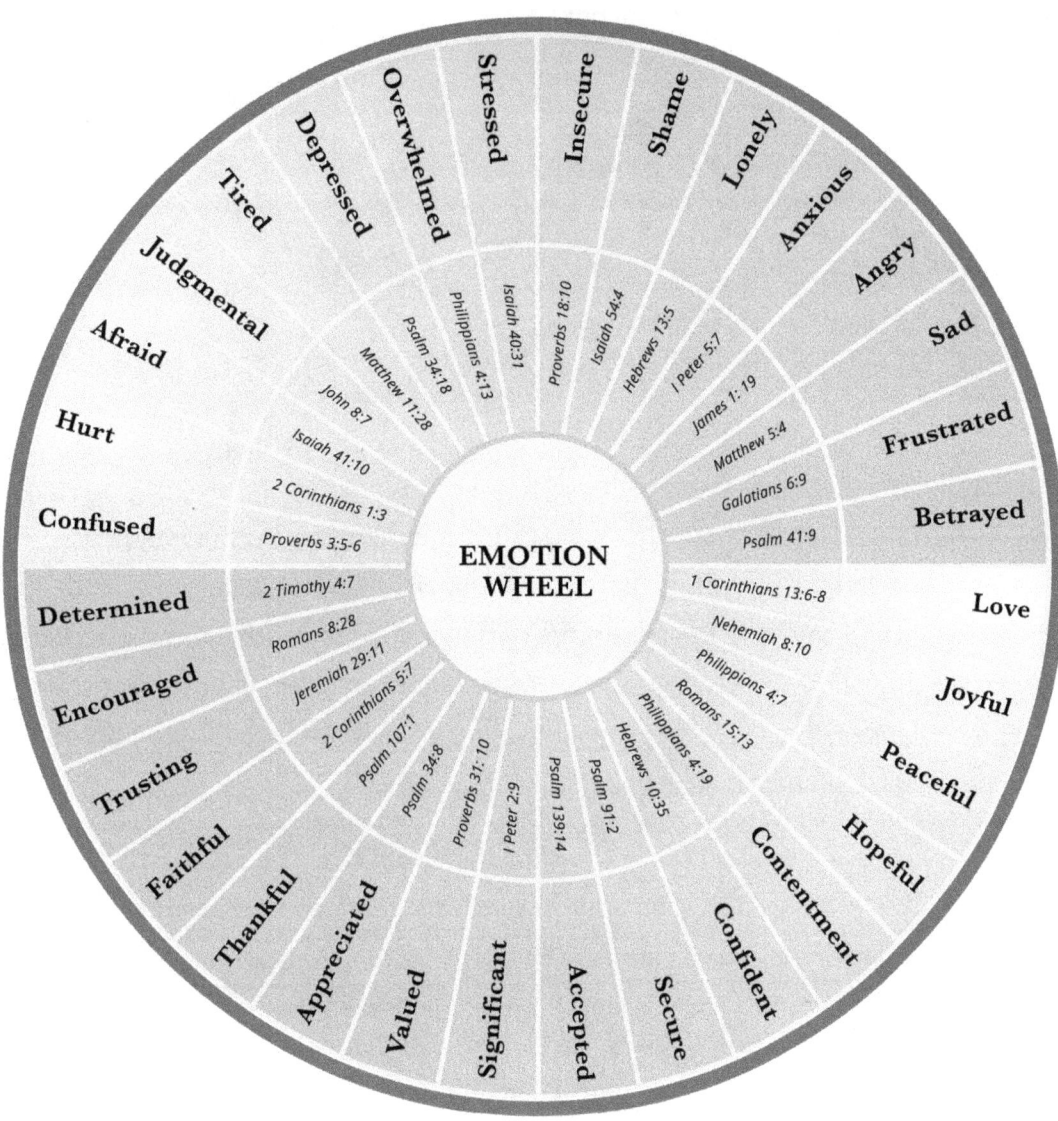

Which emotions are present for you today?

Are you surprised by any of these feelings?

How do you feel about your husband?

I want you to write a letter to your husband bringing to light the truth about how he has hurt you and broken your trust. Write about all the events, memories, and emotional pain you have felt. Describe what has happened to you since you discovered his infidelity. The purpose of this letter is to face your pain. When you confront your husband with the truth you can begin your healing journey. Be specific and honest regarding what his sin has done to you.

On the next pages you will find space to write your letter. When you're finished, make a copy to give to your husband at an appropriate time (perhaps when he has agreed to a disclosure conversation, which I address in lesson 5). You are giving your husband an opportunity to feel the impact of his sin, show godly remorse, and change. Regardless of his response, you have spoken the truth in love and you will continue healing. This confrontation is based on God's command in Matthew 18:15:

> *If your brother sins, go and show him his fault in private;*
> *if he listens to you, you have won your brother.*

[All scriptures in this workbook are taken from the
New American Standard Bible Version or the King James Version.]

If you think he might cause you additional emotional or verbal harm, or physical harm, then of course do not give him the letter.

LETTER TO MY HUSBAND

How do you feel about writing this letter?

Now look at the Emotion Wheel again on page 21.

How do you feel about God right now? Don't be frightened by this question. Many women are very angry at God when their husbands betray them. They wonder why God allowed it to happen. Then they feel guilty because it's hard to admit they are angry at God. Let me share some good news: God is big and strong! He can handle your anger or frustration at Him and will not judge you for it.

Looking clearly at these strong emotions helps you heal them. Go ahead and let your feelings out. Write a letter to God in the space on the next page and let Him know exactly how you feel about the situation and Him. Just like getting the poison out of a bee sting, get all those feelings out on paper to start your healing journey.

DEAR GOD, I FEEL...

Now that you have talked with God about how you feel, let's hear from Him. In Jeremiah 29:11 He said,

> *"For I know the plans I have for you, not for calamity but for your welfare, so you can have a future and a hope."*

I love that verse! I kept it nearby when I was recovering from my husband's betrayal and it never failed to comfort me. Let's look at it together:

How does your current situation feel like a calamity?

Is calamity God's will for you?

What promise does God make to you in this verse?

God is looking out for your welfare, your well-being. He has plans for your future. You do have a future and can hope that it will be brighter than today. It will be! You can't know God's plans for your future, but you can trust and believe that those plans are for your good, not for more pain and suffering.

My prayer for you is that you will grow in your trust in the Lord. Build a wall of faith around you with these words. Faith is not faith until it is tested. You are going through a terrible trial right now, but God wants to draw you to Him. He will see you through this time in your life if you will hold on to His hand. Take courage that you can and will rise above this pain with God's help. It will all come out right. I've seen the hand of the Lord in my life and in the lives of my clients. He never fails and always provides a better future.

Now that you know God has plans for your future, how do you feel, and why?

Supportive and Unsupportive People

It is important to know who you can count on in times of trouble and who will bring you more pain. There are people who love you, will encourage you, and will pray for you.

What are some characteristics of people who are supportive?

Make a list of people in your life who are supportive, and why you can trust them:

There are people who will give you unwanted advice, gossip about your situation, or make you feel small. They are not supportive! You do not have to spend time or energy on them while you are healing.

What are some characteristics of unsupportive people?

If there are any unsupportive people in your life, what can you do to protect yourself from them during this vulnerable time?

What can you do to get more time and support from the supportive people you know?

Setting Initial Boundaries

Creating safe and appropriate boundaries after a betrayal is a challenging task. You can be in so much pain that you feel tender and easily wounded, grow a hardened heart just to protect yourself, or revel in telling others your victim story, staying stuck in it and unable to move on.

We will work more on boundaries later in the workbook. For now think of them as a fence – they keep the good in and the bad out. The bad includes any kind of abuse – physical, verbal, or emotional.

Has your safety been honored by your husband in these areas:

- Physically?
- Verbally?
- Emotionally?
- Do you feel safe in your home?
- Do you feel safe when alone with him?

Have you violated his safety in any of these areas:

- Physically?
- Verbally?
- Emotionally?

It is very common for women to feel terribly angry when they have been betrayed by their husbands. Anger is healthy because it causes you to act. However, in times of anger you or your husband might do or say things that cross a line and become abusive.

If you feel you have been abused in any way, it is important for you to tell a trustworthy person and get the support you need. There are many resources in each community to help and support you, or to give you shelter if you need to get away from a dangerous situation.

If you have violated your husband's boundaries and expressed sinful anger, you can apologize and ask forgiveness for that behavior in a way that feels safe. You can write a letter, talk by phone, or talk in person with a safe person present. Remember that your actions are your responsibility, but his actions belong to him.

Do you need to take any actions to ensure your safety?

Who can you turn to for safety?

What is the first step you will take to feel safe?

Final Thoughts

What have you discovered about your situation?

What have you discovered about yourself?

What have you discovered about God?

Thank you for working through these questions! You have completed the first step towards your new future. I am proud of you. Remember that God has plans for you – beautiful plans for your future. You have hope! It is my prayer that you feel God's arms around you and know that He will never leave you.

Insight and Prayer

Reflect about one insight you gained from this lesson and what God taught you. Write a prayer to Him, asking for help expressing your anger in a healthy way.

Sending grace and peace,

Carol

Carol

Lesson 2
Identifying Losses

Lesson 2: Identifying Losses

In this lesson you will:

- Understand the five stages of grief
- Realize what you have lost
- Decide if you are trying to fix your husband
- Trust God's plan for a more positive future

When you discover your husband's affair, a variety of emotions can arise. Some women are furiously angry. Others feel as if they are to blame. A few worry about the shame their husbands are feeling. Some are in such terrible shock that they can't feel anything at all.

It is important to give yourself time to experience all the emotions you feel. Plan on at least a year of healing before you will feel recovered from the stresses of this situation.

Emotions are not sinful. It is not a sin to be angry at your husband, his betrayal partner, or even yourself. There are many cases in the Bible in which anger was a catalyst for change. Remember how Christ became angry at the moneychangers in the temple?

In the midst of anger, fear, shame, and anxiety, hopefully there are moments when you trust that God will heal you. Grief is generally experienced in a pattern of five stages. However, you will not experience these stages in a straight line. You might move through several stages in one day and return to an early stage the next. That is normal and expected.

It is helpful to understand these five stages so you know your experience is similar to that of others. You are not alone, nor are you crazy even if at times you feel like you're going crazy. You are going through a traumatic experience and can expect to travel through these stages of grief:

Stage 1: Denial

This is when you suspect or know something is wrong but don't want to believe it or acknowledge it in any way. I went through this stage with my husband. It just didn't feel like he was with us, even when he was at home. I knew something was wrong but I couldn't put my finger on it. The husband of one of my clients started to spend every evening working with a young female co-worker. My client didn't want to believe her husband was having an affair until it was time to evacuate their home due to a hurricane and her husband wanted to give the young lady a ride to safety instead of leaving with his family.

How have you denied your husband's affair?

In what ways have you tried to cover it up or hide it from others?

Did that denial make the situation better or worse? Why?

Stage 2: Anger

Anger can be expressed in several ways. You might become silent and withdrawn. You might get sarcastic, yell, scream, or cry. You might even be tempted to act like women in the movies and throw all your husband's possessions out the window. I remember one Father's Day when I felt terrible rage about my husband's infidelity. I was angrier than I'd ever been in my life and didn't want to be anywhere near him.

There are some Christian communities that consider anger a sin.

Ephesians 4:26 tells us, "Be angry, and yet do not sin; do not let the sun go down on your anger," so it's what you do with your anger that can be sinful, not anger itself.

How do you usually express anger?

In what situations do you find yourself getting angry at others when you are actually angry at your husband?

What are some healthy ways in which you can express your anger?

Are you ever afraid of your anger?

What steps can you take to ensure that your anger does not control you or get out of hand?

Stage 3: Bargaining

When you start to do things to improve the situation, you are in what's known as the bargaining stage. You might decide to fast or to pray every day for your marriage. You might prepare your husband's favorite meals, buy new clothing or lingerie, initiate sex more often in the way he likes, or try to be more positive and pleasant. You do something that you hope will fix the situation. A wife often takes on all the work of trying to repair the damage of her husband's behavior. I did this, and at first you probably will too. We were taught to be loving and pleasing wives, so when our husbands betray us our first thought can be that it is our fault. Please remember that he is responsible for his behavior, not you!

In what ways have you tried to bargain with your husband to get him to change?

In what ways have you tried to bargain with God to receive help?

What were you hoping would happen when you made these bargains?

How did you feel when the situation didn't change?

Stage 4: Depression

I often call this stage the "pit of despair." You will feel sad and depressed during your recovery from your husband's affair. This is to be expected. However, when you are not able to get out of bed, can't find joy in daily activities you used to enjoy, or start to lose or gain lots of weight, you might have a more serious form of depression that requires counseling or medical help to overcome.

When do you feel the most despair about your marriage?

What do you do when you are in the pit of despair?

How can you focus more on the blessings in your life even when you are in despair?

What signs might be telling you that your despair is lasting too long or becoming a problem?

Who can you turn to for professional advice, such as your physician, pastor, or counselor?

Stage 5: Acceptance

You reach the acceptance stage when you don't think about the betrayal every day. Acceptance does not mean that you approve of your husband's behavior in any way. It means that you accept that this difficult situation occurred and you begin to move past it. It can easily take up to a year to reach the acceptance stage, so give yourself plenty of time and support.

Which stage are you in today?

Based on what you have learned about these stages, are there any actions you can take to help yourself move through them to acceptance and healing?

Losses

Experiencing a husband's betrayal causes a woman to lose many things, both emotionally and physically. Let's look at some common losses together.

Emotional losses
- Loss of trust
- Loss of your partner, best friend, and the spiritual leader of your home
- Loss of respect
- Loss of self-confidence

- Loss of connection to your husband and to others
- Loss of dreams and hopes for the future

Physical losses
- Loss of health if he gave you an STD
- Weight gain or loss
- Insomnia or sleeping too much
- Panic attacks
- Stomach issues
- Headaches
- Heaviness in your chest or trouble breathing

What emotional losses are you experiencing?

What physical losses are you experiencing?

Now that you have identified your losses, let's explore how to embrace them and heal them. The first step is to surround yourself with good Christian friends. A women's Bible study group can be wonderful for you at this time. Some women isolate themselves and mourn privately. Others tell everyone they know about their situation. Both these reactions can make your recovery process more difficult. In a Bible study group you meet with other women to study and learn, not just to chat. Then you can discern who in the group you can safely tell about your situation and get support from.

Do you know of any Bible study groups in your congregation or neighborhood?

If not, who can you ask to find out about your options?

How do you feel about mourning in front of others?

How can you comfortably and safely share your pain with another woman?

The next step is to enhance your exercise routine. Exercise helps you cope with your stress and feelings of depression, and counteracts late-night binges on ice cream or potato chips. Find ways to exercise that you enjoy. You can walk, join a gym or Pilates class, or use exercise videos at home.

How often do you exercise now?

What kinds of exercise do you enjoy?

What can you do to add more physical activity to your daily routine?

Do you want to exercise with a friend or would you rather do it independently?

Finally, turn to scripture. God's word can uplift and comfort you in *any* situation.

> *The LORD is the one who goes ahead of you;*
> *He will be with you. He will not fail you or forsake you.*
> *Do not fear or be dismayed.*
> *—Deuteronomy 31:8*

> *Casting your anxiety upon Him because He cares for you.*
> *—I Peter 5:7*

> *The LORD is near to the brokenhearted and saves those*
> *who are crushed in spirit.*
> *—Psalm 34:18*

When you pass through the waters, I will be with you;
And through the rivers, they will not overflow you.
When you walk through the fire, you will not be scorched,
nor will the flame burn you.
—Isaiah 43:2

I sought the LORD and He answered me,
and delivered me from all my fears.
—Psalm 34:4

Roadblocks to Recovery

As you move through the stages of grief, any of these can keep you stuck and in pain:

- Isolation
- Not doing things you enjoy
- Avoiding your feelings by numbing them with food, alcohol, shopping, or other distractions
- Staying stuck in anger too long

Are any of these roadblocks impacting you?

What ideas do you have for moving past them?

One of the most common roadblocks to recovery is trying to fix your husband. This can include things like:

- Giving him books to read
- Spying on him to see if he is doing something wrong
- Having sex with him when you don't want to
- Checking his phone, emails, or social media accounts
- Dressing seductively to rekindle his interest in you

In what ways might you be trying to change your husband?

Only God can change a person's heart. It is not your responsibility to change your husband. If he wants to change and asks for your help, you can certainly support him, but he is the one who needs to do the work. Your focus should be on healing yourself.

Turn to the Lord

Throughout this workbook I remind you of God's love and care for you. You are significant, valued, and cherished in His eyes.

> *For I will restore you to health and I will heal you of wounds," declares the LORD, "Because they have called you an outcast, saying: 'It is Zion; no one cares for her.'" Thus says the LORD, "Behold, I will restore the fortunes of the tents of Jacob and have compassion on his dwelling places; and the city will be rebuilt on its ruin, and the palace will stand on its rightful place. From them will proceed thanksgiving, and the voice of those who celebrate; and I will multiply them and they will not be diminished; I will also honor them and they will not be insignificant. Their children also will be as formerly, and their congregation shall be established before Me; and I will punish all their oppressors. Their leader shall be one of them, and their ruler shall come forth from their midst; and I will bring him near and he shall approach Me; for who would dare to risk his life to approach Me?" declares the LORD. "You shall be My people, And I will be your God.*
>
> —Jeremiah 30:17–22

What does God say he'll do for you?

Now read Isaiah 61:1–7:

> *The Spirit of the LORD GOD is upon me, because the LORD has anointed me to bring good news to the afflicted; He has sent me to*

bind up the brokenhearted, to proclaim liberty to the captives and freedom to prisoners; to proclaim the favorable year of the LORD and the day of vengeance of our God; to comfort all who mourn; to grant to those who mourn in Zion, giving them a garland instead of ashes, the oil of gladness instead of mourning, the mantle of praise instead of a spirit of fainting. So they will be called oaks of righteousness, the planting of the LORD, that He may be glorified. Then they will rebuild the ancient ruins, they will raise up the former devastations; and they will repair the ruined cities, the desolations of many generations. Strangers will stand and pasture your flocks, and foreigners will be your farmers and your vinedressers. But you will be called the priests of the LORD; You will be spoken of as ministers of our God. You will eat the wealth of nations, and in their riches you will boast. Instead of your shame you will have a double portion, and instead of humiliation they will shout for joy over their portion. Therefore they will possess a double portion in their land, everlasting joy will be theirs.

What does this passage say about the future God has in store for you?

There are many beautiful images in these passages. Which one calls out to you now?

From Betrayal to Healing

What does God promise to do with your shame and disgrace?

How can you remember these promises when you are having a hard day?

What words of praise can you give God right now?

Insight and Prayer

Reflect about one insight you gained from this lesson and what God taught you. Write a prayer to Him.

God bless you today and always.

Sending grace and peace,

Carol

Carol

Lesson 3

Facing Anger

Lesson 3: Facing Anger

In this lesson you will:

- Learn twelve ways people express anger
- Identify anger patterns and triggers
- Recognize the difference between healthy and unhealthy anger
- Share your anger in a powerful yet godly way

Anger is an uncomfortable topic for many women. Start by inviting God to speak to your heart and provide comfort and wisdom.

Read this prayer aloud and know I am praying it with and for you:

Kind Father, we thank you for your continued love for us, Lord. You take anger seriously, and Father, you say that there is righteous anger and there is also anger that is ungodly and unhealthy for us. So, Father, help us reason together one with another on this topic. We thank you for your love, understanding, and comfort. Please open our hearts and minds to hear your message and learn to deal with anger in a way that is pleasing to you.

In Jesus's name I pray,

Amen

Many Christian women were taught to never express anger because it is sinful, and to keep a smile on their face and hide their feelings. But anger is a very normal and appropriate reaction when you discover your husband has been having an affair. There would be something amiss if you were not angry about such a deep betrayal!

This is a safe space to write about how angry you are at your husband, this situation, and even his betrayal partner, if you wish. Bring up all the anger, hurt, and damage his actions have caused. Don't hold back. Express it here so you can feel a lessening of the burden of pain you are carrying:

Expressing Anger

Now that you have purged some of your anger, let's look at common ways that people express anger. Some of these will be familiar to you and others won't. Place a checkmark next to the expressions of anger you typically use:

- Getting even
- Crying
- Withdrawing physical attention or affection
- Shutting down emotionally and feeling nothing
- Lashing out verbally – yelling, arguing, name calling, or screaming
- Extreme rage or property destruction
- Punishing someone indirectly (passive-aggressively) or through sarcasm
- Giving someone the silent treatment
- Letting depression take over
- Being physically abusive – pushing, hitting, slamming doors
- Being emotionally abusive – making someone feel crazy or inept
- Being spiritually abusive – using scripture to manipulate, control, or wound

Which of these expressions are you using in this situation?

In what ways might they be helpful?

In what ways might they be harmful?

If your husband is angry with you, how is he expressing that anger?

Do you feel safe when you or your husband express anger?

If you feel that you may be harmed or have a plan to harm someone, please immediately call a trusted friend, your pastor, a women's shelter, or 911.

What God Says

There are multiple biblical stories that describe God's anger in view of sin. He's a just God, but He's also a loving God. In Proverbs 11:21 we read,

"Assuredly, the evil man will not go unpunished, But the descendants of the righteous will be delivered."

The most important part of this passage is the phrase "the evil man will not go unpunished." Your husband has sinned against you and against God's commands to be sexually pure and keep his marriage vows. God sees his behavior as evil and you are entitled to that same opinion. This is righteous anger because it is in line with scripture. You are not sinning when you feel anger. However, you can veer into sin if you express that anger in an abusive way. You might be tempted to act out aggressively, damaging your husband's property or showing up at his workplace and creating a scene, but that is not healthy or in alignment with God's commands.

What Did You Learn about Anger?

When I was a little girl my daddy worked as a pharmacist. I loved him so much and wanted to surprise him, so one day I walked by myself to his store. I was about five years old and walked alone on a very busy street. I can still remember how happy I thought he'd be to see me. Instead he was angry with me. His face was full of fear and anger instead of happiness and surprise. At that moment I felt unimportant. Today, years later, when someone is angry with me, I return to that feeling.

What did you learn about anger when you were a little girl?

Look at The Anger Cycle on the following page. "I'm Feeling" describes how you might feel during times of conflict. "I Respond By" lists possible ways you react when angry. "I Desire to Be" explains what you want to feel instead of conflict. When I experience conflict I feel unimportant. I try to pacify other people's upset, and I want to feel connected. This tool can be very helpful in understanding yourself and your pattern.

The Anger Cycle

I'm Feeling
Confused
Unwanted
Hurt
Afraid
Powerless
Judged
Tired
Humiliated
Depressed
Overwhelmed
Rejected
Stressed
Insecure
Worthless
Shame
Alone
Unimportant
Anxious
Angry
Unhappy
Sad
Disconnected
Frustrated
Betrayed

I Respond By
Becoming passive aggressive
Withdrawing
Exaggerating
Being sarcastic
Lecturing
Exploding in anger
Silent treatment
Nagging
Defensiveness
Controlling
Becoming stubborn
Criticizing
Judging
Debating
Withholding affection
Becoming vengeful
Running away
Name calling
Pacifying
Becoming indifferent
Emotionally shutting down
Becoming self-righteous
Physical abuse
Bringing up the past

I Desire To Be
Understood
Wanted
Comforted
Safe
Strong
Given Grace
Refreshed
Cherished
Happy
Encouraged
Loved
Calm
Secure
Important
Respected
Close
Significant
Confident
Peaceful
Joyful
Hopeful
Connected
Fulfilled
Protected

What three feelings in the first list do you experience during times of conflict?

From the second list, choose the three main responses you engage in when you are angry:

Looking at the third list, select three desires you have during times of conflict:

What did you learn about yourself from this exercise?

A Healthy Formula

When you're angry it can be a struggle to communicate clearly. You can feel overcome with emotion, burst into tears, or lash out. I suggest you use this formula when expressing anger to someone:

"I feel _____ about _____.

My concerns are _____.

Next time it would be helpful if you _____. Will you do that?"

For example, let's say you have an agreement with your husband that he will call you at 5:00 pm every workday. If he does not call and returns home very late, you can say:

"I felt worried because you did not call me at five o'clock like we agreed and did not get home until seven. I was concerned that you were in a car accident or went to a strip club. Next time it would be helpful if you would call me when you are going to be late. Will you do that?"

Focusing on how you feel is much more effective than making accusations. Anytime you start a sentence with "You," you are apt to say something defensive like:

You did this _____.

You always _____.

You never _____.

These approaches are not effective as they can lead to arguments, lies, withdrawal, or the silent treatment. But no one can argue with your feelings. Starting with your feelings opens the door to productive conversations.

It can be hard to identify your emotions. Are you sad, angry, frustrated, hurt, or afraid?

To help you identify your emotions, review the Emotion Wheel in lesson 1.

List five emotions you are experiencing today:

Do you feel any of these emotions are "wrong"? Why?

You are responsible for your anger and how you express it. Anger can be expressed honestly and kindly or with an intent to wound and hurt. When you use the formula above, you take responsibility for your anger and express it in the most godly way possible.

If you have made mistakes and said things you wish you hadn't, know that God loves you and has totally forgiven you for everything in your past, present, and future. You always have His forgiveness. Hebrews 8:12 says,

> *"For I will be merciful to their iniquities,*
> *and I will remember their sins no more."*

You might want to ask your husband for forgiveness as well if you are worried that you expressed your anger in a hurtful way.

How will you ask forgiveness for any of the ways you've expressed your anger?

How do you feel about asking your husband for forgiveness?

Don't worry if you are not able to even consider this conversation at this point. If your feelings are too raw, just pray about them and wait for God to lead you.

Anger Is a Gift from God

When you feel angry, it is a signal from the Lord that something is wrong and needs your attention. When you think of anger in that context, your anger at your husband's behavior is a reasonable response to a traumatic situation.

You might have noticed that your anger ebbs and flows. Some days it seems manageable and other days it feels overwhelming.

How angry are you in this moment? Rank your anger from 1 to 10, with 10 being the highest.

When you are extremely angry, what can you do to help yourself feel a little better?

Unresolved Anger

Proverbs 30:33 says, "The churning of anger produces strife." Anger has consequences, especially anger that lingers a long time. You might have physical symptoms such as migraines or stomach upset. Relationships can be broken by unresolved anger. You might get depressed by it. Many women struggle with depression because it's anger turned towards themselves. Others become bitter and close themselves off from others. Only you can decide when your anger has gone on too long.

One of the ways to resolve your anger is to understand it clearly. Here are a few examples to consider:

- I'm angry that he spent money or bought gifts for his betrayal partner.
- I'm angry that he broke his marriage vows and my trust.
- I'm angry that he lied to me.
- I'm angry that he put my health at risk and/or gave me an STD.
- I'm angry that he rejected me.
- I'm angry that other people knew about his affair before I did.

If your sister or friend experienced any of these things, would you consider her anger reasonable?

What specifically are you angry about regarding your husband's sexual behavior?

What step can you take to help resolve some of your anger?

Pretending that you aren't angry won't help you or save your marriage. God values honesty. You have permission to feel angry and express it in a healthy way.

Again, practice using the formula to write some statements you might share with your husband about his behavior:

"I feel _____ about _____.

Here are my concerns _____.

Next time it would be helpful if you _____. Will you do that?"

Thank you for looking at your anger with me! I know it can be difficult. Remember that God provides you with the Holy Spirit to help and comfort you. The Holy Spirit helps you find the right words to say even when you're angry or afraid.

> *For the Holy Spirit will teach you, in that very hour, what you ought to say.*
> *—Luke 12:12*

Insight and Prayer

Reflect about one insight you gained from this lesson and what God taught you. Write a prayer to Him.

God bless you!

Sending grace and peace,

Carol

Carol

Lesson 4
Battling Depression

Lesson 4: Battling Depression

In this lesson you will:

- Learn to recognize the signs of depression
- Learn ways to pull yourself out of depression
- Understand that your mind is the battlefield
- Find strength and comfort in God's word

What beliefs and opinions do you have about depression?

In the previous lesson you learned that depression is anger turned inward. Depression is a very common experience for women who have been betrayed by a husband who had an affair. The key is learning how to fight it off, and when you need a physician or counselor to help you address it.

Some people have a mistaken belief that depression is a sign of weakness or spiritual lack. It is not. Depression is not a sin. It is a sign that you are going through a traumatic experience and need time to heal.

How do you feel now that you know depression is not wrong, just a sign of pain and trauma?

Signs of Depression

Depression can show up in different ways for different people. Here are some of the most common:

- **Insomnia** – this can include inability to sleep, waking in the night, or sleeping too much.
- **Hopelessness** – when you feel like nothing is ever going to change and you lose interest in your favorite activities. You find yourself using the words always, never, and forever. Statements that include these words are often untrue, but they can feel very true when you are depressed.
- **Intense sadness** – this feels like a black cloud is following you wherever you go. You might cry a lot or just feel mopey and terribly sad.
- **Withdrawal** – when you want to stay isolated. You might withdraw from friends, activities, and even from attending church. When I was suffering about my husband's affair I was invited to a friend's wedding. I just couldn't go. I also withdrew to my bedroom after dinner and couldn't concentrate to watch TV with my sons. I craved time alone.
- **Difficulty with concentration** – I remember going to the grocery store and finding it terribly hard to find and pay for a can of tuna fish. When you are depressed you find it hard to focus and can be forgetful or feel like your brain is scattered and foggy.
- **Change of eating habits** – this can be overeating and food cravings for some women and loss of appetite for others. Do you soothe yourself with ice cream, popcorn, cookies, or chips; or does the idea of food seem repulsive?
- **Suicidal thoughts** – We all have stray thoughts about what it would be like to escape our pain through suicide. If you find yourself planning to kill or harm yourself, you need immediate help. Suicide will harm your loved ones so deeply. It's not worth ending your life because of your husband's behavior. If you feel like you would be better off dead, please put this book down and call a friend, your pastor, a counselor, or 911 to get help immediately.
- **Loss of zeal for God** – this is deeply painful. You might feel unable to pray, read scripture, or worship.

Which of these symptoms of depression are most troublesome for you today?

How are they impacting your life and faith?

If depression is taking over your life, has lasted too long, or you have suicidal thoughts, please see your physician, pastor, or a Christian counselor for help. Asking for help is a sign of strength, not weakness. God gave us professionals who can help us. Depression can turn into a life-dominating emotional problem. Help is available if your depression is becoming frightening or impacting your quality of life.

How to Help Yourself Heal

Think of your depression as an illness that will get better with some care, attention, and time. These steps will help you battle depression so that it doesn't become a long-lasting problem:

Exercise: Exercising releases positive endorphins, reduces stress, and makes you feel better about yourself. Force yourself to get consistent exercise, even if you don't feel like it. Try exercising with a friend who will be your accountability partner.

How can you add exercise to your daily routine?

Who can exercise with you?

 **Prepare for sleep:** This is very important. I can't watch a TV show that is very intense or exciting right before bed. I need to take a warm bath, read, or watch something lighthearted or less intense. What helps you relax? You can try drinking chamomile or another soothing tea. Decrease your caffeine intake. Consider removing electronics from your bedroom so you won't be tempted to check email or social media right before going to bed. Make your bedroom as cozy and comfortable as you can so you can relax. Make your rest a priority.

What changes do you feel inspired to make that will help you relax and prepare for sleep?

 **Control negative thinking:** This is a very important strategy. When you're depressed, negative thinking makes it worse. Do your best to stop negative thoughts when you notice them. Pray, read scripture, listen to uplifting music, laugh with your children, count your blessings – do anything you can to keep your thinking positive.

Take a praise break. Write a list of ten things you can praise God for right this minute:

4. Eat in a healthy way: Give yourself the gift of nourishing meals that you enjoy and that are good for you. Watch your sugar intake and control your portions. Keep plenty of healthy snacks handy for in between meals.

What changes are you noticing in your eating habits?

How can you enjoy eating in a healthier way?

5. Connect with others: In lesson 1 you identified supportive people. Use that list and ensure that you reach out to them. Depression can cause you to isolate yourself, so do the opposite and spend extra time with others who will listen to you and uplift you.

Who would you like to connect with today for a phone call, lunch, walk, or movie?

⑥ Help others: This is so helpful! When you use your spiritual gifts to help others you get an instant lift yourself. You can volunteer at church, at a local charity, or at the local animal shelter. Do you have an elderly neighbor who can use some help with yardwork or just a friendly visit? You have much you can share with others.

Who comes to mind when you think about helping others?

Would you like to volunteer alone or with your children?

How can you make helping others fun?

Now that you have read this list of ways to battle depression, what three things will you do first to help yourself feel better?

Your Mind Is the Battlefield

When Christ enters your life you are given a brand new heart and a new nature, but you still have to deal with old mindsets, attitudes, and actions. Pastor Dr. Andrew Farley explains there are three distinct enemies of the mind:

**The flesh:** "In the flesh" is the way you thought, acted, and reacted before becoming a Christian – the worldly, unrenewed way of thinking. The flesh isn't you because you have been made new in Christ, but the residue of the flesh remains within you. You are at war with the flesh, but the Holy Spirit restrains you so that you can listen to His counsel. When you choose not to indulge in the flesh you stop yourself from sinning.

**Sin:** Sin lives in us like a virus and has the power to be persistent and convincing. It is the flesh's co-conspirator. Look at the truth of God's word and line it up with what your fleshly thoughts are saying – and now you have a choice. If you have Christ living in you, you have power over sin. So when the flesh strikes, God wants you to respond from your new heart, not your old heart. You have everything you need to defeat sin.

**Satan:** Satan loves to get into your head and whisper negative thoughts. He lies and tells you that everything is your fault and that you are unworthy and will never be loved. When you have a negative, unrenewed, fleshly thought you are accused by Satan. This is a spiritual attack!

Look at the chart on the following page. I call this the Put Off | Put On Blueprint. A blueprint shows how something is expected to work. The "Put Off" section describes ways you act when indulging in the flesh, and the supportive scripture. The "Put On" section lists ways you respond that reflect who you truly are as a Christian. Identify behaviors or habits in the first column that you need to change, using the scripture to understand God's message about them; and focus on replacing them with Christ-like thoughts and actions supported by the scripture noted in the chart. The pathway to recovery is to reject your former mindset and choose to listen, believe, think, and act Christ-like.

Put Off | Put On Blueprint
Ephesians 4:22-24

PUT OFF
Old Fleshly Thinking

PUT ON
New Christ-Like Thinking

Put Off	Reference	Put On	Reference
Adultery	Matthew 5:27-28	Pure Desires	Proverbs 5:15-19
Anger	Proverbs 29:22	Self-Control	Galatians 5:22-23
Bitterness	Hebrews 12:15	Tenderheartedness	Ephesians 4:32
Discontent	Job 10:1	Satisfaction	Philippians 4:11-13
Doubt	Romans 14:23	Faith	Romans 4:20-25
Easily Irritated	1 Corinthians 13:5	Not Easily Provoked	Proverbs. 19:11
Fear	Matthew 6:25-32	Trust	1 Peter 5:7
Flirtation	Proverbs 7:21	Quiet Spirit	1 Peter 3:4
Gossip	1 Timothy 5:13	Good Report	Proverbs. 15:30
Hatred	Matthew 5:22-24	Love & Kindness	1 Thessalonians 3:12
Impatience	Hebrews 10:36	Patience	James 1:2-3
Indulging in Alcohol	Ephesians 5:18	Abstinence	Proverbs 23:29-34
Jealousy	Proverbs 27:4	Trust	I Corinthians 13:4
Judging	Matthew 7:1-2	God Searches Your Heart	Psalm 139:23
Lust	1 Peter 2:11	Pure Desires	Titus 2:12
Lying	Ephesians 4:25	Speak Truth	Zechariah 8:16
Presuming the Future	Proverbs 27:1	Trusting God's Will	James 4:14-16
Pride	Proverbs 11:2	Humility	James 4:6
Profanity	Proverbs 4:24	Pure Speech	Proverbs 15:4
Retaliation	Proverbs 24:29	Returning Good for Evil	Romans 12:19-20
Strife	Proverbs 26:21	Peace	1 Peter 3:11
Stubbornness	Psalm 81:11-12	Brokenness	Psalm 51:17
Unforgiveness	Ephesians 4:32	Forgiveness	Colossians 3:13
Wrong Friends	Psalm 1:1	Godly Friends	Proverbs 13:20

What negative, fleshly thoughts are you experiencing now?

What situations trigger negative thinking for you?

Find Strength and Comfort in God's Word

The best way to fight off these enemies of your mind is to keep handy a list of powerful Bible verses that remind you that you are loved, protected, and under God's constant care. Grab your Bible and write each of these verses after the prompts (this not only gathers them conveniently in one place, but writing them down rather than just bookmarking them in your Bible etches the meaning into your mind):

2 Corinthians 5:17

Ezekiel 36:26–27

Galatians 5:16–17

Ephesians 2:10

Ephesians 4:22–24

Ephesians 6:10–11

James 1:22

What do these verses tell you personally?

Psalm 5:1–3

From Betrayal to Healing

Psalm 9:12

Psalm 138:8

Romans 8:28

Philippians 4:6–8

What do these verses tell you about God?

What is your favorite Bible verse? Record it here and jot down a few notes about why it is so meaningful to you:

O LORD my God, I cried to you for help, and You have healed me. O LORD, you have brought up my soul from Sheol; You have kept me alive, that I would not go down to the pit.
—Psalms 30:2–3

God is with you always and will restore you from the pit of depression!

Insight and Prayer

Reflect about one insight you gained from this lesson and what God taught you. Write a prayer to Him.

Sending grace and peace,

Carol

Carol

Lesson 5
Preparing for Disclosure

Lesson 5: Preparing for Disclosure

In this lesson you will learn:

- The difference between discovery and disclosure
- How to safely discuss your husband's sexual sin
- The difference between helpful and unhelpful questions
- Practical strategies for comforting yourself after disclosure
- How to lean on God even in the most painful moments

Discovery is when you initially learn of your husband's affair. *Disclosure* is when your husband admits he has been unfaithful and reveals all the facts. Disclosure includes a necessary formal procedure in which both partners sit down with a third party and have a conversation.

Every situation is unique, but often the wife discovers her husband's affair. It is rare that the wife doesn't know and her husband confesses.

I encourage you, if at all possible, to schedule a disclosure conversation, even if a significant amount of time has elapsed since the discovery of his affair. It's okay if you are hesitant or worried about it. I'm asking you to trust the process. It can be instrumental in your healing and perhaps in your husband's. I recommend it even if you have already discussed his infidelity. He might not have told you the complete truth, and you need someone there who is skilled in providing support and safety.

It is important for both of you to plan in advance to have this difficult and emotional conversation. Having an experienced and trained facilitator present, such as a counselor, pastor, or trusted third party, ensures your safety, increases the chances you'll get the truth, and provides an opportunity for your feelings to be honored and validated. This conversation should be held in a neutral place such as your counselor's or pastor's office. Disclosures are common in marriage counseling, and there is a process for them that keeps the conversation on track and ensures both sides are heard and feel safe.

Have you and your husband had a disclosure conversation; and if so, what was that experience like for you?

If not, how do you feel about scheduling a disclosure conversation:

- Skeptical?
- Anxious?
- Fearful?
- Relieved?
- Overwhelmed?
- Vulnerable?

Describe your feelings here:

Who can you ask to lead the disclosure meeting?

If you don't know who to ask, where can you get a recommendation or referral?

Preparing for a Disclosure Conversation

The first thing to do in preparation for a disclosure conversation is to pray. Ask God to protect, comfort, guide, and strengthen you. You should drive separately to the disclosure meeting. Arrange for child care, if needed, so that you have 24 hours after the conversation without contact with your spouse to process your thoughts and feelings. Spend the day and/or night with a trusted friend.

Consider what details you want to know and what questions you want to ask. If you are concerned that you will be overwhelmed or forget your questions, prepare a list and give it to your facilitator to review prior to the meeting.

Asking the Right Questions

It is helpful to ask questions like:

- Where did you meet your betrayal partner?
- Do I have any affiliation with your betrayal partner?
- When did your affair begin?
- What time of day did you engage in your affair?
- Was this a one-time encounter or is it a lasting relationship?
- Have you had other affairs?
- Do I know any of these betrayal partners?

- What devices did you use to communicate with your betrayal partner?
- Is this why we stopped/increased having sex?

There are several reasons for your husband to disclose this information:

- It allows him to uncover his sin and stop hiding it.
- He faces the impact of his sin, moving him a step toward reconciliation.
- It gives him an opportunity to be open and honest and ask forgiveness.
- You learn the full extent of his sin, know what you are being asked to forgive, and feel relieved to know the truth.
- It confirms what you might have only intuited, relieving lingering suspicions. (The need to know can feel worse than not knowing.)
- It ends the constant questioning.
- Your marriage can now be rebuilt on truth.

Some women want to know intimate details, but your husband's answers are not to be used to punish him but only to clear the air between you and begin the healing process.

These are ill-advised questions:

- What's her name?
- Where does she live?
- Is she prettier/younger than me?
- What did she do for you that I didn't?
- Do you think about her when we have sex?
- What exactly did you do in bed together?
- Where did you have sex?

It can be tempting to ask about these gritty details, but that information will pain you more than help you. Focus on questions that help you discover the facts of the situation. Your facilitator should guide this process.

What are the facts you need to know?

The Impact of Disclosure

Men generally dread these conversations. They want to protect themselves and avoid trouble. They often feel shame. They typically stick to the facts and give brief answers. Some shed tears and beg for forgiveness. Others are detached, either because they are afraid they will break down or they want to get the conversation over with as soon as possible.

Women are often afraid of what they will hear but are eager to stop the deception and hear the truth at last. You might feel tearful and crushed, or relieved and empowered that you are finally getting to the bottom of this situation.

After a disclosure conversation men can feel relieved and happier than they have in a long time because the tension has been released. Your husband might suddenly feel very close to you and want to be affectionate or have sex. Or he might decide to move out immediately.

Your emotions will be moving like a roller coaster. You might be filled with desire for your husband or never want him to touch you again. You might be angry, fearful, or too overwhelmed to feel anything.

After Your Disclosure Conversation

Shortly after the disclosure conversation write another letter to your husband sharing and releasing any further pain you feel after learning the details of his betrayal. Be specific and honest regarding how you feel now that all has been disclosed. Read your letter to your husband in the presence of a trusted friend, counselor, or pastor.

MY LETTER AFTER OUR DISCLOSURE CONVERSATION

What Happens Next

I learned from Melissa Hass's book *The Journey* that there are at least four possible ways a husband responds after a disclosure meeting:

 He is sincerely remorseful and sorrowful about cheating on you and takes actions to restore trust with you. He is honest and open, exposing his sin. He ends his relationship with his betrayal partner for good. He asks for forgiveness from God and from you. He focuses anew on his relationship to God and his family. He sees a counselor, is patient with your feelings, and gives you time to process the experience and make decisions. These are the hallmarks of a man who wants to restore the marriage.

 Having admitted the details of his affair, he believes the situation is over. He doesn't believe he'll struggle any longer and gives you the impression that you should hurry up and get over it. He might return to worshipping or get back into a Bible study or men's prayer group.

 He's sorry you found out about the affair and wants to smooth over the situation. He takes you on dates, buys you jewelry or a new car, or takes you on a vacation. He doesn't really think he has a problem and seems to lay low for a while until you simmer down. He does not make an effort to increase his faith or get closer to God.

 He's angry and tight-lipped, and acts like his affair is your fault. He denies that he is sexually impure or has a full-blown sexual addiction. He tries to run away from his pain. He might move in with his betrayal partner and file for a divorce, or he might turn to drugs or alcohol, using it as Novocain because he doesn't want to feel any pain.

There are six things which the Lord hates, yes seven which are an abomination to Him. Haughty eyes, a lying tongue, hands that shed innocent blood, a heart that devises wicked plans, feet that run

*rapidly to evil, a false witness who utters lies and
one who spreads strife among his brothers.*
—Proverbs 6:16–19

You might not be able to immediately discern your husband's reaction. Watch for some these indications:

- Does he seem prideful?
- Does he continue to lie?
- Does he hurt you or damage property?
- Is his behavior different or the same?
- Does he cause strife?
- Does he engage in angry outbursts?
- Does he stop communicating with you?
- Is he secretive about his time or about using his electronic devices?
- Does he start spending more time with you and stop secreting himself with his electronic devises?
- Does he come home on time or call if he's going to be late?
- Does he schedule a date night with you?
- Does he lead you in devotionals and attend church with you?
- Does he give you breaks from household chores?
- Does he involve you in his interests and hobbies?

These reactions provide a good measuring stick. Pray and ask God to show you what you need to know. Remember that a changed heart equals changed behavior.

Do you see any positive changes in your husband's behavior?

What troublesome behaviors are continuing?

Has the strife in your home increased or decreased?

How Are You Doing?

You've covered a lot of ground in this workbook already. In what ways are you feeling better about yourself and your situation?

Do you feel closer to the Lord?

Post this Bible verse where you can see it often:

I will not leave you as orphans. I will come to you.

—John 14:18

May you feel the comforting arms of our Heavenly Father around you always.

Insight and Prayer

Reflect about one insight you gained from this lesson and what God taught you. Write a prayer to Him.

Sending grace and peace,

Carol

Carol

Lesson 6
Understanding Boundaries

Lesson 6: Understanding Boundaries

In this lesson you will learn:

- Your need for healthy boundaries
- The five temperaments
- About facing struggles with boundaries

From the book *Boundaries in Marriage* by Dr. Henry Cloud and John Townsend I learned the importance of having healthy limits. Boundaries are like property lines. They are used to protect property. Examples are fences that surround a backyard and homes protected in gated communities. Other homeowners install security cameras that safeguard their properties 24/7.

Boundaries are important in protecting a marriage, too. Your husband's infidelity was a boundary violation that caused you pain.

How have you struggled in setting healthy limits with your husband?

The Five Temperaments

When I was in my doctorate program for Clinical Christian Counseling I took a course entitled "Creation Therapy: A Biblically Based Model for Christian Counseling" by Drs. Richard and Phyllis Arno. I learned about the God-given temperaments based on Psalm 139:13–18. The five temperaments are: Melancholy, Choleric, Phlegmatic, Supine, and Sanguine.

Let's take a close look at five women, their temperaments, and some of the challenges they have in setting boundaries:

Melanie Melancholy has very deep, tender feelings, but she rarely reveals them because she doesn't want to feel vulnerable. She fears rejection and builds a wall around herself when she perceives the threat of rejection. Melanie will be devastated when she discovers that her husband has cheated on her. Because of her deep, tender feelings she might ventilate her anger in destructive ways. She might feel a need to get even because her husband has discarded her for his betrayal partner.

Chloe Choleric will likely try to manipulate her husband in vengeful ways upon learning of his affair. She might lock her heart up tight and become so self-focused that she will be difficult to reach. She will struggle with being unable to forgive, and it will be next to impossible for her to renew trust in her husband. The only emotion she will feel is anger. Chloe can become emotionally or even physically abusive. It is highly likely she will turn her back on her husband and walk away from the marriage.

Phoebe Phlegmatic will handle her husband's betrayal better than most, as she has no real fear of rejection. She will show little emotion and will actually become cool and complacent. Phoebe needs peace in her life; if she confronts her husband about his betrayal it could cause conflict and change, which she'd rather avoid. If she senses any direct conflict from her husband she'll either disregard him or defend herself with sarcasm. She can be cutting and belittling with her words.

Susan Supine desperately wants love, affection, and approval, but once she learns of her husband's infidelity her hurt will run deeply. She will feel used, unlovable, and worthless. She will say she is hurt, but what she really feels is anger. This hidden anger can quickly turn into bitterness, resentment, and depression. Susan will withdraw and alienate herself to protect herself from further pain. She can become vulnerable to abuse.

Sarah Sanguine's biggest fear is rejection. Because her husband's love and attention has been given to his betrayal partner she will likely become extremely jealous. Sarah needs a great deal of love and affection, and because she has been rejected she might completely disregard her boundaries and become impulsive. When her need for love isn't satisfied she might become hostile and explode with anger.

Which one of these women most closely describes you?

Let's look at each of these women more deeply. They all struggle to maintain healthy boundaries, though each suffers from this lack differently. When a husband is unfaithful and engaged in an affair, it's overwhelming and devastating. Melanie tries to gain revenge. Chloe experiences tremendous resentment. Phoebe keeps the peace by withdrawing. Susan hides her feelings. Sarah can easily turn her back and move on.

Temperament Recommendations

Tips for Melanie Melancholy:

- Become secure in God's love. You are worthy of His love.
- Live to please God, not others.
- Learn to forgive your husband.

Tips for Chloe Choleric:

- Submit to God and know that He will never let you down.
- Find ways to discharge your anger and stress.
- Look at your husband through the "Eyes of Christ."

Tips for Phoebe Phlegmatic:

- Connect with God and be more involved in your relationship with Him.
- Examine your behavior to see where you have been too passive or overcompensating in trying to keep the peace with your husband.
- Make decisions based on God's will.

Tips for Susan Supine:

- 💜 Recognize you are valuable and loved by God.
- 💜 Shift your dependence from your husband to God.
- 💜 Learn to express your feelings honestly instead of hiding them.

Tips for Sarah Sanguine:

- 💜 Interact with God when you are forced to be away from your husband.
- 💜 Deal with anger in ways that are pleasing to God.
- 💜 Stop to think about the consequences of your choices.

Women's Struggles with Boundaries

Rank your satisfaction with your boundaries in the following areas from 1 to 10, with 10 being the highest:

- Ensuring you are physically safe
- Access to emotional care and connection
- Communicating what you need to say
- Managing anger
- Safeguarding your freedom and fun
- Having personal responsibility and control over your life
- Guarding your personal financial security and decision-making
- Managing your time the way you choose to
- Safeguarding your relationship with God

What is one thing you can do today to set healthier boundaries in areas in which you are not satisfied?

It takes courage to look at yourself and your behavior honestly. Thank you! We are all on journeys to become the best women of God we can be, and must learn to maintain healthy boundaries.

I learned from Melissa Hass, in her book *The Journey*, that there are several boundary issues that women struggle with across the globe. Once discovering their husband's affairs, any of the women profiled above might:

- **Deceive others** – this is when you smile on the outside and tell others what they want to hear. You lie to avoid trouble or slant the truth to keep the peace and retain your dignity.

- **Send indirect signals** – for example, you expect your husband to be a mind-reader, pouting and professing that everything is fine when really you're hurt because you didn't get what you wanted.

- **Talk too much** – this is when you badmouth your husband, gossip about him, or share personal details that should be kept confidential. You tell your story to get pity from others, or out of anger seek to damage your husband's reputation.

- **Enable** – this is when you try to spare your husband pain or consequences by making excuses for his behavior.

- **Find fault** – this is when you try to control your husband through constant reminders, criticisms, or instructions.

In what ways do you find it difficult to maintain healthy boundaries in any of the above situations?

How to Proceed

The Bible gives us ideal guidance when we need to confront other people about their sinful behavior and set boundaries. Matthew 18:15-17 reads:

If your brother sins, go and show him his fault in private; if he listens to you, you've won your brother. But if he does not listen to you, take one or two more with you, so that by the mouth of two or three witnesses every fact may be confirmed. If he refuses to listen to them, tell it to the church and if he refuses to listen even to the church let him be to you as a Gentile and a tax collector.

Use these biblical guides to have difficult conversations about boundaries with your husband. Below are some great questions to ask yourself that will help you prepare:

- What is the problem?
- Is it mine, his, or do we both contribute?
- Is the problem harmful or just annoying?
- What attempts have we made in the past to resolve the problem that weren't successful?
- What are possible solutions to the problem?
- What is my obligation in working towards the solution?
- What are my options in responding to the problem?

Let's practice using these questions. Choose a boundary problem that you have with your husband. Because this is a practice exercise, use a less important problem than that of his betrayal.

What is the problem?

Is it mine, his, or do we both contribute?

Is the problem harmful or just annoying?

What attempts have we made in the past to resolve the problem that weren't successful?

What are possible solutions to the problem?

What is my obligation in working towards the solution?

What are my options in responding to the problem?

What did you learn from this exercise?

Remember that boundaries are not designed to end relationships; they are designed to preserve and deepen them.

Insight and Prayer

Reflect about one insight you gained from this lesson and what God taught you. Write a prayer to Him.

Sending grace and peace,

Carol

Carol

Lesson 7
Confronting Fears

Lesson 7: Confronting Fears

In this lesson you will:

- Recognize how fear is impacting your relationships
- Uncover the fears hidden in your heart
- Recognize unhealthy fear
- Learn to trust God to deliver you from your fear

Fear is one of the most debilitating emotions that you will encounter on your healing journey.

What has been your greatest fear since discovering your husband's affair?

That's a very profound question, as it reminds you that God is in control of everything. He will never stop loving you for any reason. How do you describe your relationship to God? Check one:

- I feel totally secure in His love.
- I trust Him but sometimes I have doubts.
- I feel like He's far away right now.
- I wonder if He really exists.

Be honest here and don't worry about being judged. We all have times when we feel very close to God and others when we feel more distant. Some of you may be searching and turning towards God during this time in your life.

What do you fear about your relationship with God?

"Fear not" is one of the most mentioned commands in the Bible, yet sometimes we struggle to trust God, especially during times of trauma. When my husband had his affair I was terribly afraid about having enough money. I'd been a stay-at-home mom and now my husband was living with his betrayal partner. I had to go back to work, but God provided for me in miraculous ways. I always had just enough.

How much do you trust God right now? Rank it from 1 to 10, with 10 being the highest.

Don't worry if your score is low. You have been betrayed by the person you loved and trusted most in the world. It's okay if you can't trust people or God right now. It will get better in time, I promise.

Common Fears

I always feel better when I know that my experience is "normal." Here are some of the typical ways that women struggle with fear after their husband betrays them:

- I did something to cause this to happen.
- I can't compete with his betrayal partner.
- I'm not loveable.
- I can never trust him again.
- He will never tell me the truth.
- All men are liars.
- Once a cheater, always a cheater.

List your fears about your marriage, your spouse, or your future here:

Will He Change?

It is impossible for you to know if your husband will change. It could be that his problem with sexual sin is a lifelong one. Will he seek God, correct his behavior, and work hard to preserve your marriage and family? The only thing you can do is wait and observe. Watch his behavior, not his words. I heard a saying long ago that I'd like you to remember: "Trying is lying." You will be able to trust him again if he demonstrates a consistent and persistent change in his behavior.

Your Mother's Heart

If you have children, you are worrying about them as well as yourself. It is a difficult topic to discuss with them, but an important one. If you have a son, are you worried that he will follow his father's example and get involved in an extramarital affair, pornography, or other sexual impurity? If you have a daughter, could there be a problem with your husband's behavior towards her? You might worry that you will have to raise your children alone or that your children will blame themselves for the rift in your marriage.

Record your worries for your children here:

Children are very observant and know when there is stress in the home. The best-case scenario is that you and your husband sit down with them and explain things in an age-appropriate way. Your husband should take the lead in this and say something like

"I have done something sinful that has broken your mother's heart. I was wrong. I was with another woman the way I should have been with Mom. I am asking God to help me, and I want you to pray for me."

If your husband refuses to take responsibility like this or has moved out, you need to explain it to your children in the best way you can. Try something like this: "Daddy is not at home right now because he has done something sinful that is very wrong. He was with another woman the way he should have been with me. We need to pray for him."

It is very important that you explain things honesty to your children in a safe and age-appropriate way. If not, they might blame themselves for your sadness or blame you for their father's absence. Your level of faith and honesty will help them feel safe. It is okay for them to know you are very sad. Take the opportunity to pray together and witness your faith during this trying time. When they know that God will take care of your family, they feel safer.

Unhealthy Fear Patterns

When you are very afraid, you can fall into beliefs and behaviors that do not support you. Are any of these true for you?:

- If I take better care of my husband he'll be faithful.
- I'm part of the problem. It's because I'm too fat, not pretty [etc.].
- I can stop my husband's unfaithfulness if I pray harder.

I have said this before and it bears repeating: You are not at fault or responsible for your husband's behavior. You cannot control him or force him to change in any way. When you have these fears, realize they are Satan's lies and take them to God. Do you feel responsible for your husband's actions? Record any feelings of responsibility here and ask God to heal you now:

God's Way of Banishing Fear

The most powerful thing you can do to ease your fears is to give them to the Lord. Psalm 34:4 is a perfect verse to plant in your heart:

> *"I sought the Lord and He answered me, and He delivered me from all my fears."*

What does this verse tell you?

Fear is Satan's tool for tormenting us. It is a demonic spirit that seeks to devour our peace of mind and tender hearts. Satan knows that when we are traumatized fear can create all kinds of havoc in our lives. But God is bigger than any fear! The way out of fear is to submit to God in prayer knowing that He has already answered that prayer and will deliver you. You can battle Satan and fear, but it requires a warrior's heart and constant connection to God in prayer and through His word.

> *Trust in the Lord with all of your heart and do not lean on your own understanding. In all your ways, acknowledge Him and He will make your paths straight.*
> *–Proverbs 3:5*

What does this verse reveal to you?

Think for a moment about your biggest fear right now. It might be that you will be rejected, judged, shamed, or cast out. It might be that you have failed or that you won't be able to support yourself financially if your husband abandons you. You might feel that your testimony is tainted and God can't use you. You might think that you will be unloved and alone for the rest of your days. Whatever it is, write it down here, then give it to God. He will solve it for you!

> *For God hath not given us the spirit of fear; but of power, and of love, and of a sound mind.*
> *—2 Timothy 1:7*

How does this verse give you hope and calm your fears?

Insight and Prayer

Reflect about one insight you gained from this lesson and what God taught you. Write a prayer to Him.

Sending grace and peace,

Carol

Carol

Lesson 8

Understanding the 'Why' of His Affair

Lesson 8: Understanding the 'Why' of His Affair

In this lesson you will:

- Learn about sexual addiction and infidelity behaviors
- Free yourself from feeling responsible for his behavior
- Let go of any false guilt
- Prepare to rebuild your marriage or move on

How do you feel about understanding why your husband betrayed you? Do you want to understand or would you rather just move on? Do you want to know every detail or do you want to avoid the topic? List your feelings here:

Whether you just want this situation to be over or you have a deep need to know more about it, the information in this lesson is designed to help you heal. It is not to excuse your husband's behavior in any way. Knowledge is power, and the information you learn in this lesson will make you wiser and more discerning.

Understanding Sexual Addiction

An addiction is a life-long pattern of behavior -- a pattern of sin that flows over many years. It develops from these avenues:

- Physical, emotional, spiritual, or sexual abuse as a child or teen
- Trauma such as parental neglect and abandonment
- Viewing pornography at an early age

Physical abuse can include violence; failure to provide safety, food, or clothing; and exposure to extreme anger. Emotional abuse can include being taught that feelings don't matter or that one is indirectly responsible for the problems in their parents' marriage. Spiritual abuse happens when ministry leaders don't confront sin through biblical teachings. Sexual abuse includes inappropriate touching and exposure to pornography.

Divorce, rejection, and even a parent's death can make children feel their parents have abandoned them. Boys can feel that they are not smart enough or talented enough to please their parents and feel a lack of love and acceptance. When boys experience these things in childhood they develop a variety of fears, which can include feeling worthless, unwanted, unloved, or insignificant.

Has your husband voiced any of these feelings?
What trauma might he have experienced as a youth?

Sexual Addiction Behaviors

When a man has a problem with sexual sin, he might engage in these behaviors:

- Fantasizing and masturbation
- Connecting with other women on social media or dating sites
- Viewing pornography
- Engaging in emotional affairs, which usually leads to sexual affairs
- Going to adult novelty stores
- Engaging in phone or video sex
- Going to strip clubs or massage parlors, or engaging escorts
- Demanding sex from you
- Changing his sexual behavior with you or asking you to do something uncomfortable
- Stopping having sex with you
- Voyeurism/peeping tom behavior
- Bestiality
- Incest or child pornography
- Rape or other criminal behavior

Sexual addiction is typically progressive. I have observed some husbands choose criminal behavior and end up in jail.

Put a checkmark by the behaviors in the list above that your husband has engaged in. Which ones hurt you the most?

Has your husband displayed brokenness and repentance before you and God?

Not everyone who is involved in sexual sin is a sexual addict. Do you know whether your husband's current affair is part of a lifelong, dominating pattern of sexual sin or is it a new behavior?

Infidelity Behaviors

These behaviors usually indicate infidelity or potential infidelity:

- Suddenly becomes critical
- Picks fights
- Becomes more interested in his appearance
- Becomes distant and emotionally unavailable
- Is late coming home from work
- Doesn't answer his phone
- Showers you with attention
- Changes his sexual activity with you
- Says another woman "is just a friend"
- Deletes his text, email, and/or search history
- Takes his calls in private
- Gets angry easily
- Becomes less affectionate
- Doesn't attend family events

Put a checkmark by the behaviors in the list above that your husband has engaged in. Which ones hurt you the most?

It is not your job to analyze your husband or decide whether or not his affair is the result of a sexual addiction, but considering these questions helps you understand the situation and possible triggers for his behavior. No matter what the triggers were, it is still his sin.

> *So then each one of us will give an account of himself to God.*
> *—Romans 14:12*

Your Response to His Struggle

When your husband is engaged in sexual sin, it is terribly painful. Have you used any of these coping mechanisms?

- Comfort from food
- "Retail therapy" (excessive shopping)
- Using drugs or alcohol to numb the pain
- Pouring an excessive amount of time into your children
- Serving others to avoid the pain at home
- Getting involved in another relationship to numb your pain

If so, how does this behavior concern you?

What changes can you make to ease this behavior?

Understanding His Fears

Now that your husband's affair has been discovered, he probably has his own fears. Here are a few common deep-seated fears he might have:

- He is unacceptable and unworthy of your love.
- He is unworthy of God's love.
- If you knew the real truth you wouldn't love him.

Because many men fear being known and judged as sinful and unlovable, they create a persona and a double life. Your husband might show you the side of himself that he believes you will accept and hide the dark parts. This deception is often the most painful thing for wives.

How do you feel about your husband after reading about what he might fear?

Does he exhibit any fear or is he showing no sorrow or fear and is actually blaming you for his affair?

Do you now feel compassion or are you even more angry? Why?

What about Intimacy?

I have observed that many men in this situation do not understand the meaning of intimacy. They believe intimacy is just sex. However, intimacy really means openness, honesty, and sharing. Were there times when you and your husband had sex and you felt he wasn't really present? How did that make you feel?

Has your husband acted out sexually with you by asking you to do things you feel uncomfortable doing? If so, how does that reflect on his view of intimacy – and yours?

If your husband has rejected you sexually or stopped having sex with you altogether, how has that affected your intimacy?

When a husband shows no desire for his wife for months and months, it is a sign he may be getting sex somewhere else or viewing pornography. Did you see signs of this in your husband before discovering his affair?

How has his behavior changed how you view sex?

How has his behavior changed your view of yourself as a sexually attractive woman?

These are very tender questions. Thank you for having the courage to answer them. Your answers will help you understand yourself better and move forward in your healing journey.

Each woman reacts differently to sexual betrayal. When my husband had his affair I was almost forty and his betrayal partner was in her twenties. I was struck by how different we were. It was so hard for me to comprehend how he could want someone who was the opposite of me when I'd tried so hard to be a good wife.

His Healing Process

It is imperative for a husband to put God's plan first in his life if he is to heal from an affair or sexual addiction. He needs to focus on his relationship with God and be 100 percent sure of his salvation. Without a belief in his salvation he doesn't have the power of the Holy Spirit residing within to restrain him from sexual sin. His heart is hard, he isn't interested in pleasing God, he has a sinful nature. He is powerless to change. He doesn't possess the mind of Christ, therefore he naturally sins.

Your husband will only experience lifelong freedom from sexual sin when his life is under the control and leadership of Jesus Christ.

> *If we confess our sins, He is faithful and righteous to forgive us our sins and to cleanse us from all unrighteousness.*
>
> *–I John 1:9*

Next he needs an accountability partner who is a strong Christian male familiar with this behavior and the lies and deception that accompany it. He needs help from a counselor who specializes in infidelity or sexual addiction. Depending on the scope of his sexual sin, he also needs support by participating in Celebrate Recovery or another Christian group-recovery program.

If your husband has sought Christian help for his sexual sin, how do you feel about this?

If he hasn't, is there anything you can do to encourage it without expressing it as an expectation that he will reject?

The Most Important Thing

Now that you understand the possible causes and triggers of sexual sin in men, do you understand that his behavior is not your fault? This is the most important thing for you to glean from this workbook. Even if you both contributed to the struggles in your marriage, his sexual sin is 100 percent his responsibility. His sexual sin isn't about you.

Can you believe that today? Why or why not? Write your thoughts below:

If He Wants to Work on the Marriage

God has a plan for your husband, despite his sin. God wants to comfort and heal him. That is God's job, not yours. You can do the following to support that healing:

- Pray for your husband.
- Set appropriate boundaries.
- Speak honestly.
- Help him see the Lord more clearly.
- Encourage him to appreciate his strengths.
- Be sure he knows that he can be forgiven.

Brethren, even if anyone is caught in any trespass, you who are spiritual, restore such a one in a spirit of gentleness; each one looking to yourself, so that you too will not be tempted. –Galatians 6:1

What can you cling to from these words of Scripture? What, if anything, do you want to change about how you relate to your husband?

If He Refuses to Work on the Marriage

God has a plan for you if your husband will not leave his betrayal partner, repent, and change. You might need to:

- Get ready for him to cut you off financially
- Open your own bank accounts
- Look for employment
- Schedule an appointment with a Christian counselor to help you prepare emotionally
- Build a support team of trustworthy friends, family members, and ministry leaders
- Make an appointment with an attorney to determine your legal rights

Remember, there is a difference between a man who is contrite and seeking to align his life with God and a man who continues in his sin without remorse. Which scenario describes your husband?

How does that make you feel?

Understanding your feelings helps you in your healing journey.

From Betrayal to Healing

Insight and Prayer

Reflect about one insight you gained from this lesson and what God taught you. Write a prayer to Him.

Sending grace and peace,

Carol

Carol

Lesson 9
Releasing Resentment

Lesson 9: Releasing Resentment

Congratulations on continuing to work on your healing journey! This is deep work that requires courage and faith. I am very proud of you.

Now that you are nine lessons into this program, how have you changed?

In this lesson you will learn how to:

- Let go of resentment
- Free yourself of the need for justice
- Give your resentment to God

What do you resent about this situation with your husband? Consider all the things you've lost and are mourning. Get all those resentments out here on paper so you can look at them:

If your husband has shown godly remorse or repentance, how do you view his sincerity?

What decisions, if any, have you made about the future of your relationship?

Whether you are clear that your marriage will end or you're still working to salvage it, resentment can be extremely toxic and painful. Releasing it doesn't mean that you forgive your husband or that you condone his actions, it just means that you are working to be healthy and whole again.

What resentments are the most troublesome for you?
Check each that apply in this list:

- That you have to manage anger
- That you desire revenge
- That you have a need to get answers to all your questions
- That you now fantasize about your husband with his betrayal partner

Why are these so troublesome for you?

What do you think you will gain if you continue to hold on to these resentments?

One of the biggest challenges is that this situation doesn't feel fair or just. You want justice and to be removed from all this pain.

What would justice look like for you?

You are at a crossroad in your healing journey. You can continue to hold on to your resentment and desire for justice, or release them. This is your decision, but you should prepare to release that load of pain at some point.

Do you feel ready to release your resentment and need for justice? Why or why not?

Remember that you can heal on your own schedule. It can take a long time to process these emotions. If you're not ready to release them today, what will help you move towards letting them go?

Give It to God

How would you feel if you could stop carrying this burden of resentment and the need for justice and could turn them over to God?

Does the idea of releasing resentment and your desire for justice to God make you feel:

- Relieved?
- Powerful?
- Trusting?
- Faithful?
- Content?
- Scared?
- Frustrated?
- Disappointed?

Why do you feel this way?

Do you believe God will provide justice for you?

> *Therefore the Lord longs to be gracious to you, and therefore He waits on high to have compassion on you. For the Lord is a God of justice; How blessed are all those who long for Him.*
> *—Isaiah 30:18*

What does this verse say to you?

When I learned of my husband's infidelity I was coincidentally teaching a lesson from the book of James at my women's Bible study group. It was entitled "How to Endure a Trial." I was not ready to release my resentment at that time, but God showed me over time that He would fight my battles for me.

> *Never take your own revenge, beloved, but leave room for the wrath of God, for it is written, "Vengeance is Mine, I will repay," says the Lord.*
> *—Romans 12:19*

What can you glean from this verse?

Some women give their resentment to God but then take it back out of pain. This can happen when you forgive too soon, before you have processed all your emotions about the situation. God needs to prepare your heart to release and forgive.

How might you fight the temptation to reclaim your resentment?

Your Journey Is Different from Your Husband's

When your husband sins sexually, God chastens him in an effort to bring him to repentance or salvation. God reveals what is hidden and brings it to the light. God does not chasten you for your husband's sins. He works to help you heal and learn to trust Him more fully.

How does this distinction make you feel?

But to me, it is a very small thing that I may be examined by you or any human court. In fact, I don't even examine myself for I am conscious of nothing against myself, yet I am not by this acquitted; but the one who examines me is the Lord. Therefore, do not go on passing judgment before the time but wait until the Lord comes who will bring to light the things hidden in the darkness and disclose the motives of men's hearts. Then each man's praise will come to him from God.
—1 Corinthians 4:3-5

Do you feel it is your job to judge your husband or punish him? Why?

When you release the burden of resentment and the desire to get even, and surrender it all to God to manage, you are rewarded with:

- Contentment
- Peace
- Freedom
- Restoration of the things you have lost

Are you ready to surrender? If not, write a prayer asking God to prepare your heart and mind so you can surrender:

If you are, write a prayer letting go of your resentment and desire for justice:

However you feel today, know that God is with you and will heal your heart over time so you can lay this burden at His feet.

Insight and Prayer

Reflect about one insight you gained from this lesson and what God taught you. Write a prayer to Him.

Sending grace and peace,

Carol

Carol

Lesson 10

Forgiving Him

Lesson 10: Forgiving Him

In this lesson you will learn:

- The nature of forgiveness
- The difference between forgiveness and reconciliation
- To free yourself from dwelling on his actions
- How forgiveness leads to your healing

> *Let no debt remain outstanding except the continuing debt to love one another.* –Romans 13:8

Forgiveness means that you absolve a debt. Your husband owes you a debt that can never be repaid. When you grant him forgiveness you release that debt, just as our Heavenly Father forgave you and dismissed your debt of sin when you asked him to.

This is a big deal. How do you feel about what you will be giving up if you forgive?

Though releasing your husband from his debt to you does not necessarily mean reconciling with him, you receive much when you forgive. Pastor Chuck Swindoll wrote, "We cannot be right with God if we are not right with others." Forgiveness is an act of grace and mercy, given not because someone deserves it but because we are called to forgive by our Lord. When we can forgive others as God has forgiven us, we reflect the character of Christ.

How do you feel when someone forgives you?

How do you feel knowing that God has totally forgiven you for your past sin, current sin, and future sin?

> *For I will be merciful to their iniquities, and I will remember their sins no more. —Hebrews 8:12*

Let's look at some ideas about forgiveness:

- You can say a prayer and forgive and rid yourself of resentment, and if you still feel resentment there is something wrong with your faith or your prayer life.
- You don't need to forgive your husband and should hold on to all your anger because he deserves it.
- You should ignore your pain and forgive him quickly.

I don't agree with any of these viewpoints. I believe that not forgiving fills your life and heart with bitterness and pain. It hurts you. But it is a process that requires time to feel your emotions fully and deal with them before forgiveness can be heartfelt.

Do you think you can ever forgive your husband for his sinful sexual behavior? Even if you don't know yet whether or not you will be able to, what reasons can you list for doing so or not doing so?

Do you feel your husband deserves your forgiveness?

What You Give Up When You Forgive

I learned a great deal about the freedom forgiveness brings from June Hunt's words in *Biblical Counseling Keys: Forgiveness – The Freedom to Let Go*. When you forgive someone, you are giving up your right to:

- Receive an apology
- Be bitter
- Get even or see him brought to justice
- Bring up the offense again to yourself, your husband, or others

Forgiveness Defined

Forgiveness is not:

- Waiting until time heals your wounds
- Letting your husband get away with sin (it's giving his sin over to God)
- Reconciliation
- Minimizing the pain of the affair
- Forgetting (we don't have the capacity to forget deep wounding; only God can do that)
- A feeling (it is a choice)

Forgiveness takes place in you alone. It:

- Is a change in your thinking about your husband's offense towards you
- Goes one way, from you to your husband
- A gift that cannot be earned

Forgiveness and Reconciliation

Reconciliation is a two-way process. It requires both you and your husband and flows between you. It requires a change in behavior from your husband and is earned when he works to rebuild trust and repair your marriage.

Forgiveness	Reconciliation
Only takes you	Takes you and your husband
Is a change in your thinking about your husband	Is a change in behavior by your husband
Can't be earned by your husband	Must be earned by your husband
Is a gift to your husband	Is extended to you through your husband's efforts

How do you feel about forgiving your husband now that you know the difference between forgiveness and reconciliation?

The Three Stages of Forgiveness

There are three stages in the process of forgiving your husband for his affair. They are:

Face the sin of the affair: This happens after full disclosure. You must know what you are forgiving and face the truth of it. This is difficult and requires time.

Feel the pain: You must feel and process the pain of the betrayal. This is hard, and it hurts; but it is essential to your healing process. If you deny or ignore the pain you will not be able to heal.

Forgive your husband: Forgiveness is not a feeling. It is a choice – an act of your will based on God's command to forgive.

God makes it clear that we are required to forgive others because He knows it is good for us.

> *Be kind and compassionate to one another, forgiving each other, just as in Christ God forgave you.*
> *—Ephesians 4:32*

Two Kinds of Forgiveness

Christian psychologist Dr. David Clarke explains two kinds of forgiveness in his book *I Don't Want a Divorce*:

 **"Release forgiveness"** is when you release your forgiveness and move on. It requires no change. You don't need any contact with the other person or to even communicate your forgiveness. You are just releasing the person to God knowing He will do what needs to happen in their life.

 **"Intimacy forgiveness"** is required for reconciliation. This is when there are personal meetings between the two parties, understanding and godly remorse is shown, and behavior is changed. Both parties display kindness and empathy towards each other, and the relationship begins to heal and deepens.

Can you achieve only release forgiveness or might you also achieve intimacy forgiveness? Why?

When It's Hard to Forgive

When considering forgiveness, you can get stuck in several ways, such as:

- 💟 You think you have to wait until you feel like forgiving.
- 💟 You want to wait until you can forget about what happened.
- 💟 You want to hold on to the hurt and continue thinking about it.

Which of these ways of getting stuck are the most challenging for you, and why?

If you are struggling to forgive your husband, I understand. He has betrayed you and caused you deep pain, and it is part of your human nature to want justice and for him to suffer as much as you are. Consider it this way: You are not forgiving your husband for him, you are doing it for you. You want to obey God's commands and live in accordance with His will.

These verses will strengthen you. Underline the words that speak to you.

> *For this reason I say to you, her sins, which are many, have been forgiven, for she loved much; but he who is forgiven little, loves little.*
> *—Luke 7:47*

> *But one whom you forgive anything, I forgive also; for indeed what I have forgiven, if I have forgiven anything, I did it for your sakes in the presence of Christ so that no advantage would be taken of us by Satan, for we are not ignorant of his schemes.*
> *—2 Corinthians 2:10-11*

> *As far as the east is from the west, so far has He
> removed our transgressions from us.*
> *—Psalm 103:12*

What is in your heart now that you have read these verses?

When you forgive your husband, either with release or intimacy forgiveness, you win! You will be rewarded with joy, peace, and an assurance that God has a plan for your life. You will be able to feel the good kind of pride because you have been faithful to God's word.

If you want to forgive your husband and are struggling, try this process:

- Pray and ask God to help you forgive.
- Pray and tell God that you forgive your husband in obedience to Him.
- Pray and ask God to bring all the emotions and gifts that follow forgiveness.

This process might require some days or weeks in between each prayer, or you might be able to do it all at once. Forgiveness is the greatest healing process of all these twelve lessons. You can do this!

Now you are ready to forgive and follow God's command. You will write a letter to your husband expressing your painful emotions and describing his hurtful behavior and hurtful words and how they affected you. Be honest and direct. Get everything out. You will end the letter with the words "I forgive you." (If appropriate, you can make a copy and give it to your husband.)

MY FORGIVENESS LETTER

Insight and Prayer

Reflect about one insight you gained from this lesson and what God taught you. Write a prayer to Him.

Sending grace and peace,

Carol

Carol

Lesson 11
Rebuilding Trust

Lesson 11: Rebuilding Trust

In this lesson you will learn:

- How your husband can rebuild your trust
- Where your responsibility begins and ends
- How to create safe boundaries before problems arise
- How to rebuild your trust in yourself and in God

This lesson is all about rebuilding trust. It could be that your husband is genuinely trying to change his behavior and preserve your marriage – or not. His behavior is his choice. This lesson will help you respond to any of his behavior in a confident way, trusting that God will guide and protect you.

Based on how your husband is behaving today, how consistent are his words and actions?

You've read before that the only way to measure your husband's progress is through his behavior. He has likely spent a long time covering things up and lying to you, so it is his responsibility to now prove to you that his words and behavior are in alignment so that you can start to trust him.

How much effort do you see your husband putting into changing his behavior?

His recovery is his responsibility. There is no way you can manage or control it for him if you are to believe that he truly wants to win your trust.

Are you doing anything to manage his recovery?

How can you release that responsibility back to him?

Your husband can do some simple things to begin rebuilding your trust:

- Stop lying.
- Stop being defensive.
- Not dictate how long your recovery will take.
- Put God first in his life.
- Be on time.
- Do what he says he will do.
- Prioritize you before his work or social activities.
- Be understanding and give you space when you need it.

What evidence is there that your husband is making an effort to develop these habits?

What else can your husband do to rebuild your trust?

Openness and Truthfulness

Openness means being honest about your behavior. Truthfulness means sharing your challenges and struggles to live in accordance with God's word. Participating in men's groups and adopting accountability partners are very helpful ways for men to practice both openness and truthfulness. However, your husband must also practice these attributes at home with you.

This can be very challenging for both parties. For men who have made a practice of being deceitful, covering up their actions, and hiding their temptations and struggles, being transparent and authentic is frightening and difficult. For a wife who has been betrayed, it is hard to share personal truth and to trust that what he tells you is honest. To preserve your marriage your husband needs to learn to be open and truthful. It is a process that takes time and practice.

What evidence is there that your husband is making an effort to be transparent and authentic?

Trusting God

One of the most helpful things you can do to support your recovery is to release your husband and his recovery to God. This is challenging because you want to help, encourage, or control his process so you can feel safer. But you are also controlling and managing your own pain when you do this. You think that if you do your part he will do his, and everything will be better.

Unfortunately that doesn't work. Just as his affair and sexual sin was not your fault, his recovery belongs to him alone. He needs to work it out with God on his own. You can listen and be encouraging if you wish, but you cannot force him or move him to address his behavior. If you do the work of his recovery, you will never be able to trust that his recovery is real.

Releasing him to God is an act of extreme faith and courage. It's challenging but freeing at the same time. This release is a key to your healing.

How ready are you to release your husband and his recovery to God? Why?

Write a letter to God either releasing your husband and his recovery to His care or asking Him to give you the faith and courage to make the release soon.

MY RELEASE LETTER

From Betrayal to Healing

Beginning to Set Your Boundaries

In this exercise you are going to focus deeply on yourself. Be a detective and give this some thought.

First, in the appropriate column on the form, make a list of your husband's behaviors that are hurtful to you. These can be something as small as being distant or hiding his phone, to big things like contacting his betrayal partner or going to a strip club. Take time on this list and make it as complete as possible. It's okay if you need to work on this over a couple of days.

His behaviors	How they make me feel	My response	God's counsel

Now go back to the Emotion Wheel in lesson 1. Use it to record how each of these behaviors make you feel in the next column. For example, they might make you feel worried, sad, angry, disappointed, etc.

Next consider each situation and decide what you will do in response to such behavior. For example, if he is late coming home from work, and that makes you feel frightened that he is rekindling his affair and meeting his betrayal partner, your response will be....

Finally, find comfort from God's word and list scripture that supports your feelings and responses in the last column.

This can seem like an overwhelming assignment. It will take some time, but it is time well spent because it gives you an opportunity to think about things before they happen. In the past you were surprised by your husband's behavior and had to decide what to do in the heat of the moment. By creating this list you are setting your boundaries before anything happens. This will help you trust yourself and your judgment. You will no longer feel dominated by his behavior. Pray over your list and ask God to guide you and give you wisdom as you complete it.

This list is just a start. The ideas you put down are not set in stone. You can revise them over time as you like.

Once you have completed your list, write a letter to your husband sharing your new and renewed boundaries. Use this formula when writing your letter:

I feel _____ about _____.

My concerns are _____.

What you can do that will be helpful to me is _____.

My request is _____.

If you choose to _____ I will respond by _____.

MY BOUNDARIES LETTER

How do you feel now that you have written this letter?

God will help you grow in grace and confidence as you work with this process. You can decide when you want to share this letter with your husband. I recommend reading your "Boundaries Letter" in the presence of your counselor or pastor. Or if it feels emotionally safe you can give your husband a copy and ask to meet to discuss the letter in a few days.

This exercise is not about issuing demands or ultimatums to your spouse, but a way to let him know honestly and clearly how his behavior impacts you and how he can expect you to respond. You are making your choices very clear to him. Over time, setting clear boundaries will become second nature to you and you'll be able to do it with ease. Start slowly for now and let yourself become more comfortable with it over time. This is a big part of your recovery process.

God Is Your Refuge

The Lord appeared to her from afar, saying I have loved you with an everlasting love; therefore, I have drawn you with lovingkindness. Again, I will build you and you will be rebuilt.
—Jeremiah 31:3

Setting boundaries can bring up feelings of fear, especially if you have had to hide your feelings to keep the peace at home. God will help you. You cannot control your husband or his recovery process, but you can set clear boundaries and ask for what you need. God will build your confidence and skill in setting boundaries.

From Betrayal to Healing

Insight and Prayer

Reflect about one insight you gained from this lesson and what God taught you. Write a prayer to Him.

Sending grace and peace,

Carol

Carol

Lesson 12

Believing God

Lesson 12: Believing God

Congratulations! You are almost at the end of this workbook. I am proud of you for working so hard on your journey from betrayal to healing. Your journey does not end at this point, but you are wiser, stronger, and better equipped to move forward. God is always by your side. My prayer is that you feel more connected to Him than ever before.

In this lesson you will learn to:

- Deepen your trust in God
- Claim your identity in Christ
- Use tests to make godly decisions

How difficult is it for you to trust God, and why?

Do you believe that God is good and loves you unconditionally?

Do you believe that God's will for you won't be circumvented?

Do you remember a time when you completely surrendered yourself and your life to God? What happened?

Let's do a little digging into God's word. I love to spend time reading scripture and find immense comfort and healing in hiding God's word in my heart. The "Who Am I in Christ" list on the next page shows what the Bible reveals about God and His love for you.

Who I Am In Christ
Biblical Truths to "Practice Believing" created by Pastor Pat Conway

I AM GOD'S...
- possession - *1 Peter 2:9*
- child - *John 1:12*
- workmanship - *Ephesians 2:10*
- friend - *James 2:23*
- temple - *1 Cor 3:16*
- vessel - *2 Timothy 2:20-21*
- co-laborer - *1 Cor. 3:9*
- witness - *Acts 1:8*
- soldier - *2 Timothy 2:3*
- ambassador - *2 Cor 5:20*
- building - *1 Cor 3:9*
- husbandry - *1 Cor 3:9*
- minister/instrument - *Acts 26:16 / 1 Tim 4:5*
- chosen - *Ephesians 1:4*
- beloved - *Romans 1:7 / 2 Thess 2:13*
- precious jewel - *Malachi 3:17*
- heritage - *1 Peter 5:3*

I HAVE BEEN...
- redeemed by the blood - *Rev 5:9*
- set free from sin /condemnation - *Rom 8:1-2*
- set free from Satan's control - *Col 1:13*
- set free from Satan's kingdom - *Eph 2*
- chosen before foundation of world - *Eph 1:4*
- predestined to be like Jesus - *Ephesians 1:11*
- forgiven of all my trespasses - *Col 2:13*
- washed in the blood of the Lamb - *Rev 1:5*
- given a sound mind - *2 Timothy 1:7*
- given the Holy Spirit - *2 Cor 1:22*
- adopted into God's family - *Romans 8:15*
- justified freely by his grace - *Romans 3:24*
- given all things pertaining to life - *2 Pet 1:3*
- given great and precious promises - *2 Pet 1:4*
- given ministry of reconciliation - *2 Cor 5:18*
- authority over the power of enemy - *Lk 10:19*
- access to God - *Ephesians 3:12*
- been given wisdom - *Ephesians 1:8*

I AM...
- complete in him - *Colossians 2:10*
- free forever from sin's power - *Romans 6:14*
- sanctified - *1 Cor 6:11*
- meet for the Master's use - *2 Timothy 2:21*
- loved eternally - *1 Peter 1:5*
- eternally kept in the palm of his hand - *Jn 10:29*
- kept from falling - *Jude 1:24*
- kept by the power of God - *1 Peter 1:5*
- not condemned - *Romans 8:1-2*
- one with the Lord - *1 Cor 6:17*
- on my way to heaven - *John 14:6*
- quickened by his mighty power - *Eph 2:1*
- seated in heavenly places - *Eph 1:3*
- the head and not the tail - *Deut 28:13*
- light in the darkness - *Matthew 5:14*
- candle in a dark place - *Matthew 5:15*
- city set on a hill - *Matthew 5:14*
- salt of the earth - *Matthew 5:13*
- his sheep - *Ps 23 / Psalms 100:3/ John 10:14*
- a citizen of heaven - *1 Peter 2:11*
- hidden with Christ in God - *Psalms 32:7*
- protected from the evil one - *2 Thess. 3.3*
- kept by the power of God - *1 Peter 1:5*
- secure in Christ - *Jn 10:28-29*
- set on a Rock - *Psalms 40:2*
- more-than-a-conqueror - *Romans 8:37*
- born again - *1 Peter 1:23*
- a victor - *1 John 5:4*
- healed by his stripes - *Is 53:5*
- covered by blood of Jesus - *Rev 12:11, 1 Pet 1:19*
- sheltered under his wing - *Psalms 91:4*
- hidden in secret place of the Almighty - *Ps 91:1*

I HAVE...
- access to the Father - *Romans 5:2*
- a home in heaven waiting for me - *Jn 14:1-2*
- all things in Christ - *2 Cor 5:17*
- a living hope - *1 Peter 1:3*
- an anchor to my soul - *Hebrews 6:19*
- a hope that is sure and steadfast - *Heb 6:19*
- authority to tread on serpents - *Luke 10:19*
- power to witness - *Acts 1:8*
- the tongue of the learned - *Isaiah 50:4*
- the mind of Christ - *1 Cor 2:16*
- boldness and access - *Hebrews 10:19*
- peace with God - *Romans 5:1*
- faith as a grain of mustard seed - *Luke 17:6*

I CAN...
- do all things through Christ - *Philp 4:13*
- find mercy and grace to help - *Heb 4:16*
- come boldly to the throne of grace - *Heb 4:16*
- quench all the fiery darts - *Eph 6:16*
- tread on the serpent - *Luke 10:19*
- declare liberty to captives - *Isaiah 61:1*
- pray always and everywhere - *Luke 21:36*
- chase a thousand - *Joshua 23:10*
- defeat (overcome) the enemy - *Rev 12:11*
- tread Satan under foot - *Rom 16:20*

I CANNOT...
- be separated from God's love - *Rom 8:35-39*
- be perish or be lost - *John 10:28, John 3:16*
- be moved - *Psalms 16:8*
- be taken out of my Father's hand - *John 10:29*
- be charged or accused - *Romans 8:33*
- be condemned - *1 Cor 11:32*

The Benefit of Using This List

Satan is a liar and the father of it. He deceives the nations and deceives Christians into thinking his lies are true. He is the accuser of the brethren, who accuses us before the throne of God. Zechariah 3:4 depicts the scene before the throne of God where the saint stands in tattered garments and Satan at his right hand making incessant accusations against him. The Lord steps in by commanding the angel of the Lord to clothe him in new garments clean and white, to put on him a turban. And the Lord declared:

> *"I have caused your iniquity to pass from you, and I will clothe you with change of raiment."*

The Revelation of Jesus Christ declares (Revelation 3:5, Revelation 3:18, Revelation 4:4) that the saints are clothed in white raiment that the shame of their nakedness does not appear.

- **Revelation 3:5** - He that overcometh, the same shall be clothed in white raiment; and I will not blot out his name out of the book of life, but I will confess his name before my Father, and before his angels.
- **Revelation 3:18** - I counsel thee to buy of me gold tried in the fire, that thou mayest be rich; and white raiment, that thou mayest be clothed, and that the shame of thy nakedness do not appear; and anoint thine eyes with eyesalve, that thou mayest see.
- **Revelation 4:4** - And round about the throne were four and twenty seats: and upon the seats I saw four and twenty elders sitting, clothed in white raiment; and they had on their heads crowns of gold.

Revelation 12:10 declares that *"the accuser of our brothers is cast down, who accused them before the throne day and night."*

Romans 8:33 is even more emphatic when it says, *"Who shall lay anything to the charge of God's elect? It is God that justifies. Who is he that condemns? It is Christ who died, rose again, and sits at the right hand of God making intercession for us."*

Too often believers believe the lies and accusations of the enemy. They either are ignorant of what God has said or they willingly disbelieve it based on their "feelings." We do not need to feel anything! God's truth is God's truth. *"Let God be true and every man a liar."* (Romans 3:4)

We need to learn who we are in Christ and confess the same out loud. I am what God says I am regardless of how I feel about myself. My feelings cannot change the absolute truth of God's word. We need to see ourselves in the light of God's word. Once we have heard and seen God's truth we are to RECKON it to be so. *"Likewise reckon ye also yourselves to be dead indeed unto sin, but alive unto God through Jesus Christ our Lord."* – Romans 6:11. The word reckon is "logizomai" in Greek, which means to calculate, count it up, logically sum it up as so. Sum up what God says as true and leave the rest.

From Betrayal to Healing

Using your Bible, return to *Who I Am in Christ* and look first at the list of what/who you are to God and read the entire verse or the phrase that speaks to you. Record it below.

I am God's:

Work through the remaining lists in the same way. Let your eyes capture a description, then read the full verse in your Bible and record it here:

I have been:

I am:

I have:

I can:

I cannot:

Review the verses you selected. What do they say to you in this moment?

Consider memorizing these verses in order to hide them in your heart. Return to this list anytime you want to deepen your connection to God. It will always give you new insight and wisdom.

Measuring Progress

How have you grown while working through these lessons?

What do you want to praise God for?

Describe to what extent you have been able to surrender your husband and marriage to God:

How often do you turn to God for guidance and wisdom?

I can do all things through Christ who strengthens me.

–Philippians 4:13

What does this verse mean to you?

In what ways has your husband shown true godly remorse for his sexual sin?

In what ways has he changed his behavior?

If He Is Unrepentant

My husband left me for his betrayal partner. He ended our marriage. I had no control or choice in the matter. Some of you are with an unrepentant spouse who wants to stay married and keep on sinning.

> *Yet if the unbelieving one leaves, let him leave;*
> *the brother or the sister is not under bondage in such cases,*
> *but God has called us to peace.*
> *—I Corinthians 7:15*

> *The prudent see danger and take refuge.*
> *—Proverbs 27:12*

What do these verses tell you?

I firmly believe that if your physical, emotional, or spiritual well-being is threatened by your husband's habitual sinning, you are free to separate from him. God does not call us to bondage but to peace.

Divorce

Divorce and remarriage are very hotly debated issues. Each religious denomination has its own stance. Even pastors and seminary professors offer differing opinions, which can be so confusing. But God is not the author of confusion. He gives each of us discernment and free will. I believe that God speaks to each of us through scripture and gives us the perfect guidance for our situation.

How to Make Godly Decisions

I learned from June Hunt's *Biblical Counseling Keys: Decision-Making – Discerning the Will of God* that there are eight scriptural ways to test a decision to see if it aligns with God's will. They are:

 Scriptual test: Has God already spoken about it in His word?

 Secrecy test: Would it bother me if everyone knew about this decision?

 Survey test: Would I want others to follow my example?

 Spiritual test: Am I being led by the Holy Spirit or am I being pressured by others?

 Stumbling test: Will my actions cause another to sin?

 Serenity test: Have I prayed about this decision and does it bring me a feeling of peace?

 Sanctification test: Will this decision keep me growing as a child of God?

 Supreme test: Will this decision glorify God?

Use these decision tests whenever you need to make a decision. They are particularly helpful when you must make a painful decision, like deciding to separate.

> *Do not be anxious about anything, but instead, by prayer and petition, with thanksgiving present your request to God, and the peace of God that surpasses all understanding will guard your heart and mind in Christ Jesus.*
> *—Philippians 4:6-7*

What decisions do you want to take to God today?

Ask Him for guidance here:

> *But we all, with unveiled face, beholding as in a mirror the glory of the Lord, are being transformed into the same image from glory to glory, just as from the Lord, the Spirit.*
> *—2 Corinthians 3:18*

How is God's image increasing in your life?

When Does the Journey End?

When your thoughts and conversation are no longer focused on your husband's betrayal, your most painful mourning is over and you have reached acceptance and peace.

How close are you now to acceptance and peace?

The pathway from betrayal to healing is an individual journey full of twists and turns, progress and setbacks – but it ultimately leads to joy. You don't walk this path alone. God is with you, drawing you, leading you, teaching you, and comforting you every step of the way.

> *And I am sure that He who began a good work in you will bring it to completion at the day of Jesus Christ.*
> *–Philippians 1:6*

Insight and Prayer

Reflect about one insight you gained from this lesson and what God taught you. Write a prayer to God, thanking Him for His work in your life and asking for continued healing, discernment, and a return of joy and peace.

Parting Words

My sister in betrayal, if you have been looking for God on this journey, the most important message I can leave you with is that God loves you and wants a relationship with you. He wants you to trust His love. During our time together you might have realized that you made some mistakes early on. I made them too. In Romans 3:23 God says, "All have sinned and fall short of the glory of God."

God sent Jesus to pay for your sin and is extending you forgiveness.

> *For the wages of sin is death, but the free gift of God is eternal life in Christ Jesus our Lord.*
> *—Romans 6:23*

> *To accept Jesus and become a Christian you simply agree by faith that Christ died for your sin according to the scriptures, that He was buried, and that He was raised on the third day according to the scriptures.*
> *—I Corinthians 15:3–4*

> *If you confess your sin, He is faithful and just to cleanse you of your sin and all unrighteousness.*
> *—I John 1:9*

I invite you to admit you've sinned, believe, and receive Christ's total forgiveness. Upon accepting this invitation you will:

- Have peace and fellowship with God
- Be ready for heaven
- Receive a new heart where Christ takes up residence
- Be empowered by the Holy Spirit
- Begin to understand scripture
- Have everything you need for life and godly living

If you are ready to receive true love and forgiveness I invite you to pray this prayer:

Dear God,

Through my experience of betrayal I'm finally ready to receive Jesus's love. I recognize He died for all my sins. I'm a sister in betrayal who wants to become a sister in Christ. I want rest for my soul. Today I receive His gift of total forgiveness and accept Him as my Savior and Lord. I am giving my life to you and I receive your unending love.

In Jesus's name,

Amen

And this is my prayer for you:

Kind Father:

I come to your throne room of grace and mercy bringing my beloved sister before you. On her journey of betrayal I pray she has felt your tender touch, knowing that you bind up and heal the brokenhearted. May she be gentle with herself, knowing she is not alone in her grief. You promise you will never leave her nor forsake her. My prayer is that she will be given wisdom, knowledge, understanding, and discernment regarding the next step she is to take in her marriage and in life. May you bless her and keep her, holding her up with your righteous right hand. Thank you, Father, for giving her peace that surpasses all understanding and guarding her heart and mind in Christ Jesus.

In Jesus's name I pray,

Amen

Thank you for sharing part of your journey with me. May you be blessed with joy, hope, and an abundant faith.

Sending grace and peace,

Carol

Carol Erb, Ph. D.

ABOUT THE AUTHOR

Carol Erb, Ph.D., is a board certified Christian counselor and marriage coach, a national speaker, and author of *Enveloped*. She is the creator of *From Betrayal to Healing*, a comprehensive online program for women, especially Christian women, who have been betrayed by a husband's affair. Women from the United States and beyond seek her counsel by joining self-guided and group programs and private, one-on-one video sessions.

Carol offers a leader's training program through which leaders receive a commission when individuals purchase the program directly. These comprehensive programs fit any budget and are designed as alternatives to counseling. Women who work through the twelve weeks of healing are more likely to rebuild their confidence, reignite their faith, and remove their fear of the future so they can trust their decisions and take the next right step in their marriages and their lives.

Carol's broad range of personal and professional experiences equips her to address each unique woman's struggle, and she has a reputation for saving marriages. Hundreds subscribe to her free report, *8 Proven Strategies for Recovering from a Husband's Affair*, at www.drcarolerb.com. She has been featured and interviewed in magazines and on radio and television.

Carol received her master's in Christian counseling from Southeastern Seminary followed by earning her Ph.D. in clinical Christian counseling from Cornerstone University. She opened her private practice in 2010. She and her husband currently live in coastal South Carolina, where she enjoys flower gardening, bird watching, and kayaking. She likes to travel and try unique dishes. She admits she's a coffee snob!

Carol loves everything coffee… lattes, frappuccinos, coffee ice cream, and tiramisu. When she's not working with clients, she enjoys making memories with friends and family.

Connect with Carol

On the Web:

www.drcarolerb.com

For information about Carol's From Betrayal to Healing programs:

https://betrayaltohealing.com/programs

For speaking opportunities:

hello@drcarolerb.com

Follow Carol:

Facebook: https://www.facebook.com/drcarolerb

Instagram: https://www.instagram.com/drcarolerb

LinkedIn: www.linkedin.com/in/carol-erb-85b73215

Twitter: https://twitter.com/CarolErb

MY NOTES

www.ingramcontent.com/pod-product-compliance
Lightning Source LLC
Chambersburg PA
CBHW081919170426
43200CB00014B/2772